The Lords of
Cardiff Castle

The Lords of Cardiff Castle

CHARLES GLENN

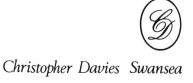

Christopher Davies Swansea

© Charles Glenn

Christopher Davies (Publishers) Ltd
Published in 1976 by
Christopher Davies (Publishers) Ltd
4/5 Thomas Row
Swansea SA1 1NJ

ISBN 07154 0301 X

*Printed in Wales by
Salesbury Press Ltd
Llandybie, Dyfed*

*Original photographs with acknowledgement
to
Neil Jones, Cardiff City Parks Department*

CONTENTS

Introduction to the Roman Period   7
The Remote Stronghold of Rome   9
Introduction to the Norman Period   15
Fitzhamon's Motte   19
Robert the Consul   26
William Fitzcount   35
The Lords of Clare   39
Introduction to the Edwardian Age   48
The Castle Builders   51
The Despensers, the Supreme Royalists   62
Introduction to the 15th Century   74
The Beauchamps and the Nevilles   77
The Plantagenets   85
The Coming of the Herberts   89
The Tudors   95
The Herbert Earls of Pembroke   99
Introduction to the Bute Period   117
The Marquesses of Bute   120

APPENDICES

1   Roman Castrum Development   148
2   Norman Castle Development   149
3   West Wall Development   150
4   The Changing Face of the West Wall   152

Introduction to the Roman Period

Before the Romans came, Britain was peopled by the descendants of races of three main types.

There were the early Stone-Age men, somewhat racially similar to the Eskimoes, and like them hunters. They came to Britain, then part of the mainland of Europe, in pursuit of their prey.

Later, when Britain had become a separate island, they were joined by the Neolithic, the New Stone-Age, men, who used implements of stone of a more advanced type as well as of bone and hörn. They brought with them domestic animals, including dogs, sheep, goats and pigs. They were skilled in primitive forms of agriculture using the antlers of deer, shed annually, as spades. They were short, dark, long-headed people like some living in the Pyrenees and the remoter areas of Wales, to-day.

The Bronze-Age men, racially similar but culturally more advanced, joined them later. All these peoples, collectively, are known as Iberians, being thought to have originated from the Iberian area of the Mediterranian.

They all appear to have lived at peace with one another spending their lives in their different habitats for the most part, but meeting occasionally, acquiring from each other articles of commerce and specialised skills.

Around 500 B.C., the first waves of the war-like Iron-Age men, the Aryan Celts, invaded Britain from France, or to use its earlier name, from Gaul. These were followed at irregular intervals by others of their race, the last of them the Belgae tribes from Belgium, the fiercest of them all, arriving only one hundred years, or so, before the Romans made their first abortive attempt to conquer Britain.

Although ruthless, the Belgae did not succeed in exterminating the earlier settlers because, like other, later, conquerors, they took captives, the men for slaves and the women to mother their children. Their descendants were the so-called Ancient Britons who defended their island against the might of Rome.

They were a rude, barbarous people dwelling in primitive hutments built in forest clearings. They practiced strange religious rites, including human sacrifice. They burned, rather than buried their dead. The elaborate Burial Chambers, such as the one at Tinkinswood in Glamorganshire, belongs to a much earlier age.

Their war paint was blue; a dye from the leaves of the woad, a mustard tree. They enslaved their enemies and used them as merchandise, exchanging them for other goods. Trade was carried on with the Continent although the volume was small. Nevertheless, it was infinitely greater than the trade carried on between the various tribes in other parts of the country.

This was because it was much more difficult then to transport goods across a land of almost impenetrable forests without roads than it was by sea, hazardous though voyages to distant lands were. It is for this same reason that it is thought that after having conquered England, the Romans arrived by sea, rather than across country, for their final and, ultimately, successful assault on the coastal low lands of South Wales.

CHAPTER ONE

The Remote Stronghold of Rome

Rome was not built in a day and neither was Cardiff Castle its remote stronghold. From its siting by the Taff, nearly two thousand years ago, the original fortress was built, rebuilt and modified according to the needs of the times, and of its occupants, some of the most powerful families in British history.

Despite the fact that the Castle has been lived in almost continuously since Norman times, it was not known until the late nineteenth century that it had been a Roman Castrum.

"I came, I saw, I conquered," was the proud boast of Julius Caesar after his victory over the Pompeians but he did not find it so easy in 55 B.C. He came and saw Britain, but he did not conquer. A year later he tried and failed again.

Indeed, nearly a century was to pass before the Romans were to succeed. In 43 A.D., Aulus Plautius with 40,000 men, took advantage of inter-tribal conflict, and invaded and conquered Britain up to a line connecting the Wash to the Severn.

Beyond that frontier, especially in the hilly country on the borders of Wales, conditions proved much more difficult. So much so that the Romans abandoned plans for further conquests and attempted to consolidate their gains.

Their hopes for peaceful co-existence with the native tribes, however, proved ill-founded. Caractacus had organised the Silurian tribes of South Wales into an effective resistance force and harassed them, looting their settlements. Their position became untenable. They were forced to withdraw or to fight on in terrain where all the advantages lay with the defenders and where even Apollo, their great Sun god, so often deserted them, vanquished by storm clouds and mist.

They attacked. Their losses were considerable, but calling on

9

reserves they triumphed at last. Caractacus was captured and sent a prisoner to Rome. Even then they were not left in peace. The persistent hostility of the tribes compelled them to build in South Wales one of the three strongholds they established and maintained permanently in Britain. They called it "Isca Silurum", and sited it at Caerleon, a place name derived from the Latin, "Castra Legionum" meaning Camp of the Legion. It became the headquarters of the second Augustan Legion, consisting of approximately 5,000-6,000 armed men.

Nothing is known for certain about Cardiff Castle in Roman times. There are no records and no complete excavation has ever been attempted. Nevertheless, deductions have been made from the extensive Roman remains found largely by accident in the late nineteenth and early twentieth centuries. From these it is evident that a castrum, defended by earthern banks existed beside the River Taff from about 76 A.D. It consisted of an

The Roman Wall.

almost square site with high banks and, probably, timber stockades.

Pirate raiders from Ireland, a menace to the Roman settlements, were probably the reason why the Castrum was built in the first place and also why it became necessary at some date between 250-300 A.D. to build stone walls beyond the banking. These walls were about ten feet thick at the bottom and five feet six inches at the top which was at least seventeen feet from the footings. These measurements are deduced from an examination of the masonry still standing. The corners were rounded on the inner side to strengthen them, and were in consequence increased in thickness, within the angle of the wall, to a maximum of sixteen feet.

Since it is known that the Romans did not use polygon bastions elsewhere until about 300 A.D., it is reasonable to suppose that those of this shape at Cardiff were not constructed before then. Furthermore, since only one of the eighteen found on the site was bonded to the wall from the base up, it is con-

Parts of the original Roman Wall seen in the South Wall of Cardiff Castle.

sidered that most of the wall was constructed before the bastions, and probable that there was some urgency to provide some protection for the defenders along the more exposed northern and eastern sides of the camp relying meanwhile on the natural defences of the river and sea to the west and the south. When this object had been attained, the bastions were constructed separately up to the same level as the walling and from that point the building of the wall and the bastions was completed, bonding them together. The bastion, bonded from the base up, is the wall to the east of the South Gateway.

The Romans used a blue lias limestone peculiar to Penarth, which suggests that it was quarried there and brought to the site by barge which in those days could have been moored close-by along the present line of Castle Street. The sea, then, reached almost to where the walls on the south side were built and the river flowed nearby on the west.

It is reasonable to suppose that the Southgate Way of the Castrum was where the Main Entrance to the Castle is at present and that it was the water gate. A road of Roman iron-slag construction has been found there, about three feet below the present ground level, a little above sea level.

The only other means of access to the Castrum appears to have been the Northern Gateway leading to the Roman road, the "Via Julia". The roadway found there is also of iron-slag and is humped, apparently, to keep out the flood water.

Although nothing of them has yet been found, within the walls there would have been barrack blocks, storehouses, cook houses, bath houses, shrines, latrines and stables. One interesting find, in 1778, near the south-west corner of the site, was a hypocaust, which proves that Roman culture had brought the comfort of central heating to Cardiff just as it had to Caerleon, where extensive excavation activities have uncovered not only ten barrack buildings each capable of providing accommodation for a centurian and one hundred men but many other structures including an amphitheatre.

It is not likely that the military settlement at Cardiff was so complete but probable that there was a civil community centre of the type of Caerleon's Caerwent not far from Cardiff with town houses, temples, public baths, shops and inns for the use of time expired soldiery and their families as well as for those

12

who had accepted the Roman way of life and left their unsanitary settlements on fortified hilltops for the comfort and security provided by their former enemies.

In 410 A.D., the emperor, Honorius, withdrew the legions for the defence of Rome, itself, and Britain and her peoples, no longer the proud warriors they once had been, were for centuries the easy prey of barbarian invaders from other lands.

All came to loot and despoil. Some stayed and became integrated with the native peoples just as the Romans, and the Celts before them, had been. None of them, however, appear to have taken over the site of the old Roman Castrum by the Taff; none, that is, until the Normans came.

Meanwhile, during those dark ages, the fabulous King Arthur was born, at least in the imagination of men. That such a resistance leader arose in Saxon times seems certain even if

The Roman Wall.

13

Caerleon was not his Camelot, as claimed by Geoffrey of Monmouth. But whatever the truth may have been, it is a romantic thought, that if he lived, he might well have adopted, as his standard, the Red Dragon of the Roman cohort, which flies so proudly from Cardiff Castle to-day.

Introduction to the Norman Period

From the time when the Romans finally withdrew their forces from Britain, and abandoned the Castrum that had put Cardiff on the map, until the Normans came, little is known for certain of anything that might have happened in the town.

It is evident, however, that during the centuries the castle was despoiled of its fabric. Stone was removed, carried away and used for other purposes, the timber rotted, ditches filled in and eventually the proud fortress became a crumbling ruin over-grown with weeds.

Meanwhile, many men came to Britain; Picts and Scots, Angles and Saxons, Jutes, Vikings and Danes. But in spite of all these invasions, there is no evidence at present known to suggest that the old stronghold of the Romans was ever used by any other military forces, native or alien, yet there are some writers who state that it was the castle of the last prince of Glamorgan, Jestyn ap Gwrgan, in about 1030-80. They also attribute to him a coat of arms similar to that of the Earls of Clare, but with different tinctures, although, it is now accepted that Heraldry was not introduced into Britain until the second half of the twelfth century.

Many of the soldiers of Rome serving in Britain were of Saxon origin. It is reasonable to suppose that some of them remained here after the legions withdrew. Their numbers increased considerably in the mid-fifth century when Vortigen, the British ruler, menaced by the Picts, appealed to the brothers, Hengst and Horsa, to bring in mercenary Saxon troops to help him to drive them out. Having succeeded in this, the Saxons stayed on and seized land for themselves.

For stories, such as these, we are indebted to the monks, and in particular, to the Venerable Bede, who wrote the "Ecclesiastic History of the English Nation." He was a writer of great integrity, but in accepting his accounts, due allowance must be made for possible inaccuracies that they may contain due to the fact that he wrote of events more than three hundred years after they took place and that he was relying for his information on "The Destruction and Conquest of Britain," written by another monk, Gildas, living amid all the blood and slaughter of those days. He could hardly be expected to take a dispassionate view of the events of his times.

Resistance to the Saxons, threw up many British military leaders, some of Roman blood. Among the most celebrated of them to emerge was the legendary King Arthur.

Of him, too, we read much and know little with certainty for his main chronicler was Geoffrey of Monmouth, who writing in Norman times, attributed to Arthur all the characteristics and trappings of Norman knighthood hundreds of years before they were in usage.

From the pen of Geoffrey of Monmouth we have a beautiful description of the Britain he knew.

Best of islands, he called it, of unfailing plenty, with everything a man could need, abounding in metals of every kind, fields of fruitful soil yielding crops in due season, forests filled with deer, pasturage for cattle at the foot of misty mountains, sparkling springs of cool clear water, shining lakes teeming with fish, and three noble rivers, Thames, Humber and Severn, stretching out like arms to recieve ships from every land.

In Wales, this description could justifyably be used of the Vale of Glamorgan, for there, and almost nowhere else in that land of mountains, was there an area of extensive low, flat land with the deep soil suitable for such varied cultivation. Elsewhere, there is an average elevation of more than 600 feet. The old sandstone of the Brecon Beacons and the Black Mountains make those areas among the wildest and most desolate regions in the whole of Britain. The great mass of the Cambrians occupy most of the land area leaving only narrow fringes of lowland close to the sea, thus isolating the people of North and South Wales so that they are remoter from each other than they are from the folk living in neighbouring parts of England.

It was during, or soon after, the so called Arthurian period,

16

that the people of Germanic origin, the Angles, Saxon and Jutes, collectively, began to be known as the English. All the others, in the southern part of Britain, that country became known as the Land of the Welsh, or Wales.

The structure of society at that time was set out in detail in a treatise called, "The Rights and Ranks of People." It shows a rigid order of precedence from the king to the serf. The serf, or slave, was often a prisoner of war or a felon, or the child of such people, who were employed in menial tasks. Between these two extremes were the bishops and priests, thanes and churls, in that order. The thane was equivalent in rank to the baron of later times and the churl, a farmer owning land. The king had the right to call on the thane for military service and the thane, in turn, could call up his churls. Some land was tilled communally and a "Feld" as such land was called, is still to be seen at Rhossili Vile, Gower.

By the end of the tenth century England had become united under one king. In Wales, however, partly owing to geography, the barrier of the mountains, no such unity was ever achieved.

At about this time there lived in South Wales, a native prince called Morgan and his territory became known as Morganwg, or Gwladmorgan, both meaning Land of Morgan or Glamorgan. It is believed that the name of the county arose in this way.

Of Morgan's people, it is probable that some, at least, were new residents, being, perhaps Welsh immigrants from other parts of Britain, who had not, in his time, become fully integrated with the settlers of longer standing.

What is certain is that there were feuds and internal strife in the area. This is evident from the "Chronicle of the Welsh Princes" which states that in 1043 Hywel ab Owain, King of Glamorgan died, "in old age."

Yet he was no Methuselah; he had merely survived in those hazardous times to an age which we would consider normal. That his achievement was considered to be remarkable by the writer of the Chronicle is not so surprising when one reads that during the century before the Normans came, no less than thirty-five Welsh rulers had been murdered or killed in battle, another four had had their eyes gouged out and four more had died in captivity.

A slave trade flourished, too. Slaves, horses, honey, corn and malt were bartered for wines, furs, whale oil and other delicacies brought in from Ireland.

It is hardly surprising, then, that after having defeated Harold's exhausted followers, William's élite troops, recruited from all over Europe, should have gone on to conquer the coastal plains of Glamorgan where the fighting men were already engaged in deadly, internal feuds.

Though the details of their campaigns are not known, the Normans did come to Glamorgan and in settling there, gave Cardiff a new lease of life as the town awoke after the long sleep that had persisted throughout the Dark Ages.

CHAPTER TWO

Fitzhamon's Motte

Ravaged by time, the Roman Castrum was no longer a mighty fortress when the Normans came. Little remained but ruined, overgrown walls. Even the surrounding earthern banks had been reduced in size, washed away by the rains of more than six hundred years. Yet it did offer a base for the harassed invaders on a site ideal for defence.

Little is known of the manner of their coming. Neither the Normans nor the Welsh were literate and even if they had been able to write reports, they had much more urgent things to do. Consequently, such stories that we have of the events of those times were written long after they took place and were based on folklore, Norman and Welsh, and both, naturally, were biased.

Of these stories the Welsh are the more romantic. One tells of Rhys ap Tewdwr, Prince of South Wales, and Jestyn ap Gwrgan, Lord of Glamorgan, and of their quarrel over Jestyn's beautiful wife. This resulted in a deadly feud and the departure of Einion ap Collwyn to seek aid for Jestyn at the court of King William, Rufus the Red.

Einon returned with Robert Fitzhamon, his twelve knights and their feudal dependants, who met and defeated Rhys. He was slain and buried at a place, since called Pen Rhys, between Brecon and Glamorgan.

Fitzhamon received the gold that he had been promised, which had been placed along the stretch of the Cowbridge to Bridgend road, known as the Golden Mile. He prepared to return to Bristol.

Einon, however, had not been paid for his services. His price was the hand of Jestyn's lovely daughter. Incensed, he persuaded Fitzhamon to fight again. The second battle was

The Golden Lion on a Blue Shield. Attributed to Robert Fitzhamon although the early Normans did not bear personal armorial shields.

19

fought on heath land at Mynydd Bwchan near Cardiff. Again Fitzhamon triumphed. Jestyn, defeated, fled from the field.

Having thus effectively removed all native opposition, Fitzhamon stayed on in Wales and became the first Norman Lord of Glamorgan.

This story must be true in part but it is not the whole truth and nothing but the truth. It has been embellished by the imagination of generations of bards for the entertainment of noble households all over Wales.

What seems certain is that the Normans had plans for the conquest of Wales as soon as they had completed their campaigns in England and their occupation there had become an established fact.

As early as 1081, William the Conqueror made a pilgrimage to St. Davids and while there entered into a political agreement with Rhys ap Tewdwr. It is likely that he passed through Cardiff at that time but did not engage in any military activity there.

It was his son and successor, Rufus, who encouraged his earls, including Fitzhamon, granting them licences to enjoy, as princes, any lands that they were able to take possession of by force of arms. He preferred the Marches, the borderlands between England and Wales, to be held by men of his own race, rather than by hostile Welsh princes.

The first Norman marcher lord of Glamorgan described himself as, "Sir Robert Fitzhamon, by the grace of God, Prince of Glamorgan, Earl of Corboile, Baron of Thorigny, and of Grandville, Lord of Gloucester, Bristol, Tewkesbury and Cardiff, Conqueror of Wales, near kinsman of the King, and General of his Army in France." They were all grand titles, but the one he placed first, the one that gave him most pride, was "Prince of Glamorgan," and there was a very good reason for this.

In the feudal age of William the Conqueror all land in England was held by him as a vassal of the King of France, to whom he paid homage.

Although vassals of the Conqueror, and later of his son, for the lands they held in England, Fitzhamon, and the small exclusive band of marcher lords were of a very different status in Wales. There, they had conquered under licence and had all

the rights and privileges of the Welsh princes they had super-
ceded. They were responsible to no one, not even to the king,
himself.

The new lord of Glamorgan took for himself the lands by the
River Taff at Cardiff and distributed other parts of his lordship
to his twelve knights and to Einon ap Collwyn in proportion to
his assessment of the service each had rendered.

According to the system they became his vasssals and paid
for their land grants, not by money payments, but by service.
The value of the land was calculated in terms of a knight's fee.

It meant that one knight with horse and accoutrements was
to be available to serve at the castle of the lord, or elsewhere at
his direction, for an agreed number of days each year. Although
the standard varied from place to place and from time to time,
the period was commonly of a forty day duration.

The consideration for the estates granted by Fitzhamon
varied from tenant to tenant based on the quantity and quality
of the land held. Thus, Sir William de Londres, as lord of the

An Aquatint of the Mound and Keep. J. G.
Spurgeon.
(National Museum of Wales).

21

manor of Ogmore was obliged to provide the services of four knights, whereas Sir William le Soore for his manor of St. Fagans and Peterston was required to send only one.

Fitzhamon made his Motte, or stronghold, on the site of the old Roman Castrum and his knights built smaller castles or fortified manor houses on their lands.

The "Motte" was a Norman defensive development unknown in Roman times. It was at once the medieval early warning system and a stronghold. Its main feature was a lofty tower built on a hill providing an observation post from which hostile activities could be seen over a wide area, and a last refuge for the garrison.

As there was no natural high land on the old Roman site, the Normans raised an artificial mound about forty feet high, in the north-west corner, and surrounded it with a moat thirty feet wide. A wooden stockade and a tower was then built on top of the mound.

On the ground level, within the outer defences, consisting, at first, of no more than the remains of the old Roman banking and walls, was the Bailey. There the living quarters of the garrison were built.

It seems certain that after the motte and the bailey were completed the outer defences were strengthened by raising the height of the banking.

Just as the earth from the moat had been used to build the artificial mound for the motte, so gravel dug outside the banking to make a dyke was used to increase the height of the Roman banking.

This is assumed because excavation has shown that the present banking consists of two very different types of soil which were separated by a distinct line of dark mould. The lower part, built apparently in Roman times, was of a fine texture, the top soil of long ago, whereas the rest was of coarse gravel such as might have come from the ditches. It was this material used by the Normans which covered the remains of the old Roman walling, preserving it so that it lay hidden until rediscovered by chance eight hundred years later.

The lower part of the banking was found to contain pieces of iron-slag, fragments of pottery and coins of the first, second and third centuries, confirming the view that the site was in

22

The view of Cardiff, taken northward from the Keep.

23

Roman occupation from very early times. Some similar objects were discovered nearer the top in the banking attributed to the Normans. From this, and the fact that no banking now exists on the west and south-western sides of the Castle, it may be assumed that soil from banks originally there was carried across the site and used to augment the banking along the more vulnerable sides, building it up to the height of approximately twenty seven feet.

In normal times, Fitzhamon, his wife and daughter, as well as the garrison had living quarters in the bailey. There would have been many other essential buildings as well, including wooden houses for stores, and stables. Only after the outer defences had been breached would the Keep, the wooden tower on the artificial mound, be used for anything but a look-out tower. Then, all would retire across the drawbridge over the moat where, within the palisade, other wooden buildings would be used for shelter.

Cardiff Castle, essentially a military building became, as the residence of the lord of Glamorgan, the seat of local government, and the place where wrong-doers were brought for trial and punishment. From it trading licences were granted and taxes levied and collected. It was a fortress, an arsenal, a town hall, a court of law, a treasury as well as a home.

Fitzhamon, kinsman of the king, spent much of his time in the royal household and during his absences from the lordship of Glamorgan, he delegated his authority to others. He is said to have been with Rufus in the New Forest on the day he was killed.

The story told is that a priest, greatly troubled, came to Fitzhamon, stating that he had had a dream or a vision. In it, he had seen the King die. He entreated Fitzhamon to warn the King of his impending doom. This he did. Nevertheless, Rufus went hunting the red deer and was killed by an arrow. No one knows whether he died by accident or whether he was the victim of a plot. Some say it was a political assassination, others that he was sacrificed in a ritualistic rite and that his royal blood was spilled to ensure the fertility of the soil.

Fitzhamon married Sybil, daughter of Robert de Montgomery, Earl of Arundel and had one daughter, Mabel, who became his heiress when he died in 1107.

General of the army of King Henry, the younger brother and successor of Rufus, he fell mortally wounded at the Battle of Fallaise in Normandy. He was brought home and buried at Tewkesbury in the Abbey he had founded there.

CHAPTER THREE

Robert the Consul

Under the Norman kings, property passed according to primogeniture and so, provided there was a son, there was no difficulty at all. The eldest inherited his parent's property as soon as they were dead and he was twenty-one.

If there were daughters and no sons, the position was a little more complicated. Each was entitled to an equal share and came into possession of it as soon as she reached her majority or, earlier, if she married while still an infant in law. Meanwhile, the king administered the estate and acted as guardian. This applied equally whether the property devolved upon an heir or an heiress.

When Robert Fitzhamon died, Henry I administered his estate and Mabel became the King's ward. Soon afterwards, she became his daughter-in-law as well. This was because, exercising his right as her guardian, he chose his own illegitimate son, Robert, as her husband.

The King's son was a man of rare talents. Like his father, appropriately, nicknamed "Beauclerq" he could read and write. He was also a great patron of letters and so, when Geoffrey of Monmouth, who became Bishop of St. Asaphs, wrote his famous, "Histories of British Kings" he dedicated them to Robert. The "Histories", which included the legends of King Arthur, were largely fictional, but were, for centuries, accepted as authentic.

Robert became Earl of Gloucester and, by right of his wife, lord of Glamorgan and master of Cardiff Castle.

According to tradition his mother was Ness ap Rhys, daughter of Tudor, the Welsh Prince, and he, the man of two nations, was bi-lingual. He had sympathy for the aspirations of

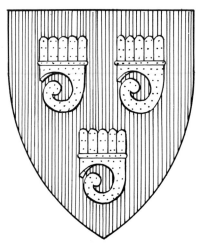

Three Golden Clarions on red. Attributed to Robert Consul and his son.

both Norman and Welshman and did much to bring about an understanding between the two races.

The Keep and Bridge, south view.

He was anxious, too, to establish law and order within his lordship and to bring sanity into a legal system so complicated that it lacked uniformity and equity.

There were two courts and those who successfully claimed the right to be tried in the Bishop's Court, could get away with murder, for it had no authority to award the death sentence, which was the perogative of the Earl's Court, alone. The cry, "Right of Clergy," then, was like exhibiting "C.D." plates on cars, to-day; clergy, even their most menial servants, too, could claim exemption from trial in the Bishop's Court, just as consulate staff now avoid answering for their offences in the courts of this country. Criminals became monks, then, solely in order to avoid punishment.

To put an end to this abuse, Earl Robert agreed principles of procedure with the Bishop of Llandaff. The treaty that they made, was considered to be so important, that it was witnessed by the leading English barons and the King of Scotland, in the presence of Henry I, himself. These principles were later incorporated into the Constitutions of Clarence, by which Henry II sought to ensure that churchmen found guilty in their own courts, were afterwards brought before the royal courts where adequate punishment could be awarded. It was resistance to these measures that lead to Thomas à Becket's quarrel with the King and his ultimate fate, and death, in his Cathedral at Canterbury.

Of local interest were rules drawn up in connection with the 'Ordeals.' These barbaric forms of the legal process of those times, included duelling in the belief that God would give the victory to the just man, lay or clerical. It was noticed, however, that in practice, almost inevitably, divine providence appeared to favour the dueller fighting on his own home ground, surrounded by his friends. It was decreed, therefore, that all duels in future should be fought at a neutral meeting place in order that there could be a minimum of interference with God's judgement by human agency.

Duelling was to be considered lawful, only if it took place in the grounds of Cardiff Castle, under proper supervision, unless both contestants were churchmen. If they were, Llandaff Fields was to be used.

Other forms of the 'Ordeal' were by fire or by water. These too were to be permitted only at the lawful venue. Those entailing the use of heat were to be performed at Llandaff. They included the 'Ordeals' by which an accused man's re-action to walking on red-hot ploughshares, or plunging his arm into boiling water established his guilt or innocence. Likewise, those where the test consisted of the suspected criminal being thrown into deep cold water were lawful only if the moat or the river close to the Castle were used.

Because of his skill and diplomacy in such matters, the lord of Glamorgan became known as "Robert the Consul."

In 1129 he founded the Benedictine Priory of St. James and there, to-day, can be seen his tomb. The church is the earliest example of Norman architecture in Bristol. He was engaged at that time in the construction of Bristol Castle, which was eventually destroyed by order of Cromwell. For this huge project, stone was imported from Caen in Normandy, and as an act

of grace, Robert devoted every tenth stone to enable the friars to build their Lady Chapel nearby.

The Keep, west view.

It is likely that, at about the same time, he undertook the conversion of Cardiff Castle, following the successful attacks of the Welsh on a number of Norman Castles, which they had discovered could be destroyed by fire. Grufydd ap Rhys had destroyed the outworks of the castle of Henry Beaumont and William de Londre's Oystermouth castle, including the tower, had been completely burnt.

At Cardiff, Robert Consul replaced the wooden palisade and tower with the massive thirty feet tall Shell Keep of stone that still dominates the site, to the north-west, on the forty feet high mound. It is a hollow twelve sided structure of stone walling six feet thick, seventy seven feet across from side to side, originally built with no apertures at all. Surmounting the Keep a rampart walk was formed with a parapet wall on its outer side, only.

It is reached by way of a small stair in the thickness of the walling on the western side of the Keep, itself.

Inside it, supported by corbels and beam holes around the

29

walls, were erected wooden buildings fronting a spacious courtyard. The Keep was strongly defended with a drawbridge across the moat, a portcullis and a guard room. Like the wooden structure it replaced, it was used only as a last refuge in case of siege. At all other times the lord, his family and the garrison, continued to live on the lower level of the Bailey, where the earlier wooden structures were gradually replaced by buildings of stone.

Robert Consul is also believed to have built the great south wall and the wall on the west of the bailey. Both of them followed the line of, and were built on the ruins of, the old Roman walls. Of these considerable areas of the original facing still exists and the core, to an average height of twenty six feet is, in part, refaced by Norman work. Some of the original Roman blue lias limestone was used, intermixed with pebbles from the river. The finished wall was ten feet thick. The bastion features of the Roman period were discarded, and protection for the defenders was provided along the top of the wall by the construction of a rampart walk with parapets on both sides.

Inside the Keep, and the Shell Keep.

30

Within the Keep there was a well. There was also a dungeon, and shortly after it was constructed, it was occupied by a very distinguished prisoner. He was Robert, Duke of Normandy, eldest son of William the Conqueror and Robert Consul's uncle.

The Black Tower

31

He had been captured in 1106 at the Battle of Tinchebrai, when he had been defeated by his younger brother, Henry I of England. Taken first to Bristol Castle, where he remained until 1126, he was then transferred to Cardiff, following, according to one account an attempt to escape, after which he had his eyes gouged out.

Since, however, it is also said that he wrote verses extolling the view from the Keep at Cardiff, obviously both stories

The Black Tower, L. Hughe, lithograph, c.1860.
(National Museum of Wales).

The Fireplace, Banqueting Hall.

cannot be true. He died, still a prisoner in 1134 and was entombed in great state in Gloucester Cathedral.

Henry I had only two legitimate children, William and Matilda. The Prince was drowned with his half-sister, the Countess of Perche, when the famous "White Ship" foundered between Normandy and England.

33

As the King lay dying in 1135, he nominated his daughter to succeed him. Each of his barons, including his nephew, Stephen swore to accept her as queen. Nevertheless, immediately after the King died, Stephen was crowned, and civil war was the result.

For twelve years, until he died, Robert Consul, on behalf of his half-sister, Matilda, waged war on Stephen.

This epic struggle so fascinated the third Marquess of Bute, lord of the Castle over seven hundred years later, that when he redecorated the Banqueting Hall, scenes from the life of Robert Consul were used, exclusively, as the subjects of the mural paintings. More than twenty pictures in all, they follow his career from his wedding in about the year 1110 to his funeral in 1147. They show him in battle both in victory and defeat, capturing Stephen and, himself, being taken prisoner.

Above the fireplace, too, he is represented in stone, a mounted figure leaving for battle. His uncle is shown behind bars, and waving him God-speed from the turreted Castle Gateway is his wife and his priest, Geoffrey of Monmouth.

CHAPTER FOUR

William Fitzcount

William, the son of Robert the Consul, succeeded as Earl of Gloucester and lord of Glamorgan. And just as his father was sometimes called, "Fitzroy," son of the king, so he is known as "Fitzcount," son of the count.

He was not so famous as either his grandfather or his father, for he was neither a conqueror or the greatest soldier of his age. He was, nevertheless, an eminent man of considerable influence.

He married Hawise, daughter of Robert Belmont, Earl of Leicester, and one of the two Justiciars of England, appointed by the King to act for him during his frequent absences abroad. Ruling, as he did, a vast territory stretching from the Pyrenees to the Scottish border, Henry II, son of Matilda and successor of Stephen, spent as much time in France as he did in England.

Earl William is remembered for fostering trade and developing Kenfig into a large and flourishing port, and for his benefactions to the Church. He was generous to his friends but somewhat careless of the rights of native Welsh chieftains who still controlled the hilly country in Glamorgan. These qualities might well have cost him his life.

The story is that he gave part of the forest of Morgan Newton, situated between Dynas Powys and Porthcawl, to his friend, Sir Richard de Cardiff. Ivor Bach, the local chieftain, claimed that the land was his.

The outcome was that the small, but resolute, Ivor, took action. He stormed Cardiff castle by night. Despite the many paid and armed retainers who filled the town, and the garrison of 120 men as well as archers, he forced his way in to the castle, using scaling ladders and ropes. Seizing the Earl, his wife and

A stained glass portrait of King John.

his son, he carried them off to his fastness in the hills, believed to have been the Castell Coch, the ancient red castle restored in the nineteenth century by William Burgess, the architect of the third Marquess of Bute.

36

There, he held the Earl and his family to ransom. He did not release them until the land in dispute had been restored to him and a large sum in compensation paid. According to tradition, the bargain was sealed by the marriage of Ivor's daughter to the Earl's son, who died when still young in 1166.

William, himself, died seventeen years later. He left three daughters as co-heiresses of his estate. Each of them married a nobleman of the highest rank. Mabel's husband was the Earl of Evreux, Amecia's, Sir Richard de Clare, and Avice became the wife of John of Mortain, the youngest son of the King. Through her, John became lord of Glamorgan and master of Cardiff Castle.

He succeeded his brother, Richard the Lionheart, as king in 1199. King John then divorced his cousin, Avice, and married Isabella of Angouleme, but he did not relinquish her property until fourteen years after the dissolution of the marriage.

It was in 1214 that the estates passed to Geoffrey de Mandeville, Earl of Essex, when that wealthy noblemen paid John the sum of 20,000 marks for the privilege of marrying Avice. He then became lord of Glamorgan but had the misfortune two years later to be killed in a tournament in London. It can hardly be said that he had value for money.

The Mandevilles were a tough family. Geoffrey's namesake though not a blood relation, for the later Earls of Essex assumed the name, was a descendant of one of the companions of William the Conqueror.

In Robert Consul's civil war he had supported Stephen until Matilda offered him greater inducements. In a remarkable covenant, witnessed by the Consul, she undertook that no treaty for peace would be entered into by herself with the citizens of London, who had offended de Mandeville, without his consent.

During the course of the war, he was forced to surrender the Tower of London, which he held on behalf of Matilda as constable, as well as his own castles at Walden and Blessey. Thereupon, he plundered the abbeys of St. Albans and Ramsey, stealing their treasures and ornaments in order to sell them for the money to pay his soldiers.

In consequence, he was excommunicated by the Pope and so could not be buried in consecrated ground. This raised a pro-

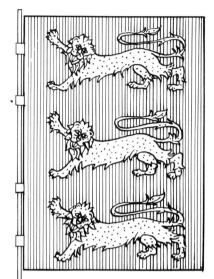

King John's Banner. Three Golden Lions on red, symbol of British Royalty was first adopted by Richard the Lionheart. It is possible they were previously used by William, Earl of Gloucester.

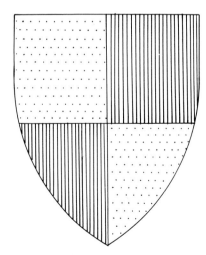

Quartered shield, gold and red, borne by Geoffrey de Mandeville.

blem for his fellow Knights Templar when he died, soon afterwards, from an arrow shot through the head.

They solved the problem, temporarily, by placing his body in a coffin of lead and suspending it above the ground by a rope tied to the branch of a tree in the orchard of their Temple Church in London. There it stayed until the Pope, in his mercy, removed the prohibition and allowed burial to take place with Christian rites.

King John, too, died in 1216, one year before Avice. She was succeeded in the Lordship by her nephew, Gilbert de Clare.

CHAPTER FIVE

The Lords of Clare

The Clares were a rich and powerful family. Like William, himself, they were descendants from the Duke of Normandy and had the Viking fighting qualities of their remoter ancestors. Among their number were martial figures like Richard de Clare, Earl of Pembroke, known as "Strongbow," the conqueror of Ireland in the days of Henry II.

Their banner, the three chevrons of red on a golden field, is one of the oldest and most famous in heraldry and is still in use by families proud of their Clare kinship.

A similar one, but with silver chevrons on red, traditionally associated with Jestyn ap Gwrgan, the last of the Celtic Princes of Glamorgan, is shown, held by the red dragon on the arms adopted by Cardiff when granted city status in 1905.

Gilbert de Clare was already Earl of Hertford when he became lord of Glamorgan and Earl of Gloucester as successor of his aunt, Avice, in possession of the lordship and Cardiff Castle.

Paradoxically, he had no estates in either of his earldoms of Hertford or Gloucester, but vast possessions elsewhere, including the family seat at Clare in Suffolk.

During the next century, four of the lords of Clare were to rule in Glamorgan and, of them, three were called, Gilbert. Despite recurrent challenges to their authority by both English kings and Welsh princes, they succeeded in maintaining their rights and privileges as marcher lords within the lordship.

Gilbert was one of the twenty-five barons appointed to enforce the observance of Magna Carta, as his father, Richard had been.

Having opposed King John, he continued to fight on the side

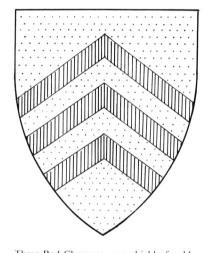

Three Red Chevrons on a shield of gold. The Arms of De Clare.

of the barons in their struggle with that king's son and successor, Henry III. As a result of which, he was taken prisoner at the Battle of Lincoln by William Marshall, Earl of Pembroke, the young king's Regent.

Eventually he made his peace, was released and married Isabel, the Regent's daughter and co-heiress. By her he had several children.

Gilbert de Clare had close family ties with the Welsh princes, for his great-aunt had married Calwalder ap Griffith, Prince of North Wales and his own sister, Joan, was the wife of Rhys-Grig, Prince of South Wales. Despite this, he was in almost constant conflict with Llywelyn ap Iorwerth, better known as "Llewelyn the Great," as well as with the lesser chieftains, Morgan ap Owen and Morgan Gam.

In 1224, Neath Abbey was pillaged. This outrage was followed by the burning of two granges where the servants were murdered and the stock stolen.

It was a situation that called for strong action. Gilbert took it. Morgan Gam was captured and sent to London in irons where he remained a prisoner in the Tower for five years. Only after hostages had been given to guarantee his future good behaviour was he released.

The disputes that called for intervention by the Lord of Glamorgan were many and not exclusively between the Welsh and the English. Some of them were family quarrels, as when Hywel ap Meredith, Lord of Miskin, gouged out the eyes of his cousin.

In 1230, Gilbert died, leaving his eldest son, Richard, then only eight years old, to succeed him.

Pending his twenty-first birthday, the lordship was held in ward and the King appointed Hubert de Burgh as Richard's guardian.

According to some writers, Hubert had married Richard's aunt, Avice, the widow of Geoffrey de Mandeville, but, if so, it must have been a very short marriage as Avice died soon after Geoffrey.

Hubert de Burgh, Earl of Kent, was Justiciar of England and has been described as the most powerful subject in Europe.

He had many duties elsewhere and in the absence of a strong lord at Cardiff Castle, once again in South Wales unruly elements were active. Although hostages, whose lives were in jeopardy, were still held in London, Morgan Gam resumed his attacks on life and property. He laid siege to Neath Castle, taking and burning it.

Stained glass portrait of Hubert de Burgh (right).

He died in 1240, the same year as the Great Llywelyn, and was buried at Margam.

Richard de Clare came of age in 1243, had possession of his lands and during the same year married, Margaret, the daughter of his guardian, Hubert de Burgh. He divorced her

Stained glass portrait of Elizabeth de Burgh.

soon afterwards, however, by order of the King, for by then Hubert was out of the royal favour, and John de Lacy, Earl of Lincoln, was in.

Shortly afterwards, the Earl of Lincoln's daughter Maud, became the wife of Richard de Clare. In this, too, the King had a hand. For his services as marriage broker, the King received the sum of 5,000 marks from the bride's father, as well as remission of a debt of 2,000 marks. Like his father, Henry III was not adverse to earning money in this way.

The new lord of Glamorgan was a vigorous man and found his time fully occupied in maintaining order not only in South Wales but on the wider national scene as well.

In 1242, he was obliged to go to the assistance of Gilbert Turberville, who was being menaced by the combined forces of Hywel ap Meredith and Rhys ap Griffiths, the lords of Miskin and Senghenydd. Having defeated them, he took hostages and held them in Cardiff Castle. Then, when Meredith persisted with his unlawful pursuits, he had him evicted from his lordship and confiscated his estates.

He took similar action against the turbulent Norman baron, Richard Syward. Being ordered to appear before the Earl's Court, on a charge of raising a war in the land against the Lord's Peace, Syward ignored the summons and appealed to the king. The lord of Glamorgan, as a marcher lord, maintained that no one, not even the king, had any jurisdiction over him in affairs concerning Glamorgan. He succeeded in his claim and forfeited the Syward estates, taking both Llanblethian and Tal-y-fan into his own hands.

Periodically, there were other outbreaks of violence. Stephen Bauzan was killed during a reverse suffered by Norman forces at Llandeilo. There was yet another attack on Neath Castle soon afterwards. Patrick de Chaworth, the husband of Hawisia de Londres, heiress of Ogmore and Kidwelly, was slain. A force of 800 mail-clad horsemen and 7,000 footmen surged through the town, burning it right up to the castle gates.

In the first general state of discontent with the government of the King, Richard de Clare sided with Simon de Montfort, Earl of Leicester, and other disgruntled barons. Shortly before he died, however, he reverted to the side of the King.

After the aptly called, "Mad Parliament", summoned in

1258, when members frightened the King by arriving at Westminster armed, wearing their swords, de Montfort, supported by de Clare, drew up the "Provisions of Oxford." These enacted that power should be vested in fifteen barons as overlords of the Government. They were charged with vetting all measures for raising funds by taxation and for maintaining law and order.

The Provisions restricted the power of the King, which at that time was desirable, but they also limited the effectiveness of the newly elected Tenants-in-Chief members of the House. This was a retrograde step on which Richard de Clare and Simon de Montfort could not agree.

Bitterly, Simon, addressing Richard, declaimed, "With such fickle and faithless men, I care not to have aught to do. And thou, Sir Earl, the higher thou art, the more thou art bound to keep such statutes that are wholesome for the land."

The rigid observance of the sabbath was a feature of those days. While at Tewkesbury, it was reported to Richard de Clare that a Jew had fallen into a privy, but as it was Saturday, the Jewish sabbath, he was refusing to accept help to get out. De Clare, unwilling to be outdone in piety, prohibited any assistance being offered on the Sunday, the Christian sabbath. By Monday, the Jew was dead.

The death of Richard de Clare took place in 1262 in mysterious circumstances. Four years earlier, it is said that Walter de Scotenay, his chief counsellor, attempted to poison both the Earl and his brother, William. The Earl, himself, survived although he lost all his hair and nails, but in July 1262, a second plot appears to have succeeded. After a meal at the house of Peter de Savoy, an uncle of the Queen, he died, together with the Earl of Deveon and other important personages.

On the death of a great lord an inventory was made showing details of his estate. This was the Inquisition Post-Mortem, and the oldest, known to exist, is the one made when Richard de Clare died. It provides interesting information regarding the rights of lords and the terms on which land was leased by them in medieval times.

Among the assets listed are the Knight's Fees, the rents payable by service. These differ very little from those due to earlier marcher lords of Glamorgan, although, in practice, there was a

growing tendency to pay rent in money in lieu of service. In particular, it is interesting to note that some of the tenants of Richard de Clare were the descendants of Fitzhamon's knights, among whom had been Gilbert de Turberville, who had been granted the semi-independent Honour of Coity as his share of the spoils of war.

Small holdings were listed, too, some in Welsh ownership, where the rent was a "Heriot" only. This was a payment made once in a generation and took the form of a death duty. Often, it was the horse and arms of the deceased landowner, which had to be surrendered by his successor to the lord of Glamorgan.

The lordship of Glamorgan was again, for a short time, held in ward, until Richard de Clare's son, Gilbert (II) attained his majority.

45

The second of the Gilbert de Clare lords of Glamorgan was an exuberant young man, nick-named "The Red." This was as much because of his fiery nature as for the colour of his hair.

One of his first official acts was to dispossess the Welsh lord of Miskin, Howel ap Meredith, whose record included the gouging out of the eyes of his cousin and the armed aggression in company with Rhys ap Griffiths against Gilbert Turberville.

Gilbert de Clare also took an active part in the conflict which continued against the king. He was an enthusiastic supporter of the policies of Simon de Montfort to curb the royal tendencies to overspend and to favour his foreign relatives when it came to appointing ministers of state.

There had been little fighting in the civil war up to 1264 but in that year a decisive battle was fought at Lewes and the King was defeated. It says much for the prestige of the young lord of Glamorgan, that it was to him, alone, that the King was willing to surrender his sword. Among the other prisoners to be taken, were the King's son, Edward, and his uncle, Richard, King of the Romans, found hiding in a windmill.

After the battle, a government was formed under the terms of the 'Mise of Lewes' headed by the three Electors. They were Gilbert de Clare, Simon de Montfort and the Bishop of Chichester.

Under their authority, a government was formed, which included, for the first time in history, representatives from each of the principal towns, as well as the barons, the bishops and abbots.

This admirable state of affairs, unfortunately, did not last long. The people were not yet ready for such reforms and there were quarrels among the Electors, who could not agree on how the more democratic state could best function. It led to a schism.

Just as his father had done, Gilbert de Clare, and other dis-illusioned barons, became reconciled to the King and Simon de Montfort was forced from office. He joined the native Welsh princes in armed rebellion and once again a state of war ensued.

Llewelyn ap Gruffydd, known as 'Llewelyn the Last' grand-son of 'Llewelyn the Great', in alliance with de Montfort, ravaged the lordship of Glamorgan. Thereupon, Gilbert de Clare marshalled his forces and drove the rebels out.

In his retreat, Simon de Montfort was hampered by the destruction of the bridge over the River Usk and the delay this caused enabled Prince Edward to re-inforce de Clare. They forced Simon to engage them at Evesham and it was there that he was defeated and died.

The battle was won, but the war was not over for the royalists. Llewelyn the Last was very much alive and continued to harass them.

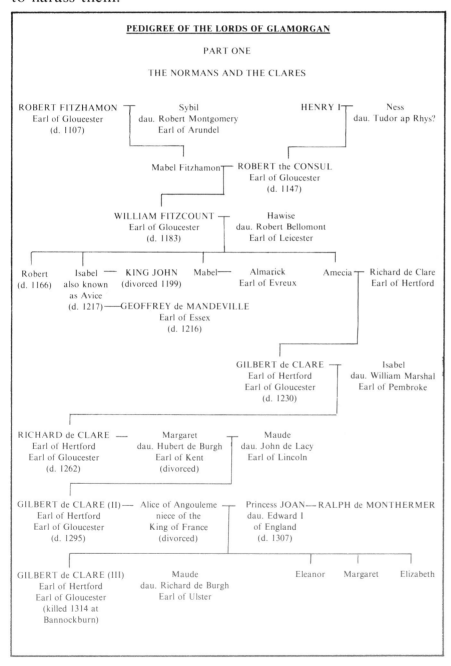

PEDIGREE OF THE LORDS OF GLAMORGAN

PART ONE

THE NORMANS AND THE CLARES

ROBERT FITZHAMON
Earl of Gloucester
(d. 1107)
— Sybil
dau. Robert Montgomery
Earl of Arundel

HENRY I — Ness
dau. Tudor ap Rhys?

Mabel Fitzhamon — ROBERT the CONSUL
Earl of Gloucester
(d. 1147)

WILLIAM FITZCOUNT — Hawise
Earl of Gloucester   dau. Robert Bellomont
(d. 1183)   Earl of Leicester

Robert   Isabel — KING JOHN   Mabel — Almarick   Amecia — Richard de Clare
(d. 1166)   also known (divorced 1199)   Earl of Evreux   Earl of Hertford
             as Avice
             (d. 1217) — GEOFFREY de MANDEVILLE
                          Earl of Essex
                          (d. 1216)

GILBERT de CLARE — Isabel
Earl of Hertford   dau. William Marshal
Earl of Gloucester   Earl of Pembroke
(d. 1230)

RICHARD de CLARE — Margaret — Maude
Earl of Hertford   dau. Hubert de Burgh   dau. John de Lacy
Earl of Gloucester   Earl of Kent   Earl of Lincoln
(d. 1262)   (divorced)

GILBERT de CLARE (II) — Alice of Angouleme — Princess JOAN — RALPH de MONTHERMER
Earl of Hertford   niece of the   dau. Edward I
Earl of Gloucester   King of France   of England
(d. 1295)   (divorced)   (d. 1307)

GILBERT de CLARE (III) — Maude   Eleanor   Margaret   Elizabeth
Earl of Hertford   dau. Richard de Burgh
Earl of Gloucester   Earl of Ulster
(killed 1314 at
Bannockburn)

Introduction to the Edwardian Age

When the Normans came, Wales had been a sparsely populated country of scattered communities living mainly on the lower foothills of the central Cambrian Mountains, in the river valleys and on those parts of the coastal lowlands where the soil was light enough for cultivation with the primitive appliances that they used.

The social structure of the Welsh was similar to the feudal system of the Normans and even more rigidly maintained. It had, too, a wider spread in status for, in addition to castes common to the more advanced nations there was a slave class.

At the top of the social structure was a king or a prince, depending on the size of the community. He lived in some state, maintained a body guard, and a court where justice was done. As protector and guardian of law and order, he expected, and exacted, contributions from all, in service or in kind.

The slaves were the absolute property of their masters. They were prohibited from hunting, from becoming smiths, bards or priests and they were tied to their communities. If they escaped, all their goods were confiscated. They were pursued and, when captured, punished. Not until the fourth generation might they become bondsmen and, like the freemen, own land themselves.

Land was held for life and passed to the sons of a deceased father, each sharing equally, although it was common for the parental homestead to pass to the youngest son.

The lord was entitled to a payment whenever the title to property passed or a daughter married. He also demanded seasonal gifts of produce as well as services.

When the Norman lord displaced the Welsh prince, he

assumed responsibility for keeping the peace and settling disputes and expected to be recompensed just as his predecessor had been. It follows then that for the majority of the Welsh, they were no worse off under the Normans than they had been under their own princes. For the slaves, the conditions were infinitely better, for they became free as soon as they managed to reach the sanctuary of a marcher lordship. To them the Norman was a liberator.

In other respects, the Welsh were allowed to continue to live in their customary ways under their own laws.

A manorial system, new to Wales, developed, for with their more advanced techniques and better appliances the Normans were able to cultivate much of the land that had hitherto been allowed to lie fallow.

The Welsh had been and continued to be in the main a pastoral people subsisting on the flesh and the milk of the cattle which they kept on the foot-hills.

Certainly differences arose between the two communities that frequently led to bloodshed, but the struggle was mainly between two lordly classes, which of course was not new to the country for there had always been clashes for dominance.

As in the past, too, alliances were formed and rival families were united in marriage.

Llewelyn the Great, for example, married Joan, daughter of King John, and in consequence, had little difficulty in becoming the accepted overlord of lesser Welsh princes. Both in the north and the south of Wales his dominance became supreme.

Most of his children, too, married into the families of the marcher lords; the most notable being the union between his daughter, Gwladus, and Ralph Mortimer. This established the direct line from Llewelyn the Great to Charles, the Prince of Wales of to-day.

Another marriage of interest within the context of this book, was that of Isabella, daughter of William de Braose and widow of Llewelyn's son, David, who married Peter Fitz-Herbert. They were the ancestors of the Herbert family, lords of Cardiff Castle in Tudor and Stuart times.

During the lifetime of Llewelyn the Great, warfare in Wales

was merely part of the general struggle between dissatisfied barons and the kings, John and his son, Henry III.

The situation changed completely when Edward I became king. He quickly established his dominion over the baronial class and then set out to bring law and order out of the chaotic state caused by the weak rule of his father. His campaigns in Wales were opposed by the grandson and namesake of the Great Llewelyn.

CHAPTER SIX

The Age of the Castle Builders

It was the activities of Llewelyn that forced Gilbert de Clare to build up his defences. Not only did he make good the damage done, but he made drastic alterations to the Keep and re-modelled the whole castle at Cardiff. He built two new towers and great ward walls completely enclosing the bailey.

As part of the Keep, facing the south-eastern corner of the site, he built an Entrance Tower, containing living quarters, which could be used habitually and not only in times of siege as formerly.

By the Main Entrance on the southern side of the Castle site, he built the Black Tower.

Between them he constructed a great ward wall, and from the Keep, following the contour of the mound, a northern wall right up to the reconstructed west wall of the Castle. It is assumed that the north wall was built after the west wall was completed as they are not bonded together as they would have been if constructed in one operation.

These new walls created an easily defended enclosure to the west of the site. The inner ward, as this area was called, was thus isolated from the outer ward to the east of it. This inner ward was divided into an inner and a middle court. The outer court was beyond the ward wall in the outer ward, where the Shire Hall and the buildings housing the garrison were.

On both the north wall and the ward wall were rampart walks with parapets for the protection of the defenders of the Castle. Access to the inner ward was by way of a gateway defended by a tower. There was a smaller, or postern, gate situated in the ward wall nearer to the Keep. Dwarf walls were built in modern times

51

The North Gate.

to indicate the extent and situation of these old walls, which were destroyed in 1776.

Little is known about the living quarters within the Keep at that time. Only one of the original rooms remains and that has suffered many alterations in later building operations. There are now neither foundations nor ceilings to indicate the size or the shape of the rooms. The only clues are provided by the beam holes in the walls which indicate that very large timbers were used to support the floors.

It is assumed that, as in other Norman castles, the ground floor was used for storage, for kitchens and for the servant's quarters. It is probable, too, that there was a door giving access to it from the central courtyard. There is no indication that

52

there ever were any interior stairs connecting the ground and the first floor levels.

The Entrance Hall, protected by a portcullis and arrow slits, was on the first floor, and this was reached from the bailey below by way of a drawbridge across the moat and stone stairs up and over the mound. Guardrooms on both sides of the moat were in use at various times.

Above the Hall was the Solar, or living quarters of the lord and his family. They must have been cold, draughty, gloomy and unhygienic by modern standards, but provided a degree of comfort far above that enjoyed, or suffered, by most other people living then. Generally, rushes were used both to carpet the floors and to provide couches for sleeping.

No fireplaces have been found and on the lower levels there were merely slits in the walls to admit light and air. These apertures were bigger progressively on each successive floor as the danger from attackers diminished. To cover them, wooden shutters were used.

Inside the Keep.

53

Early photograph c.1865-6 of the Keep by W. Collings.
(National Museum of Wales).

Latrines, or garde-robes, as they are called in castles, were entered directly from the main rooms. They were built into the thickness of the walls just as the stairs connecting the first, second and third floors were.

From the uppermost floor, a doorway led to a rampart walk over the living quarters, and to the flat roof of the tower. This was defended by a parapet with embrasures.

The Black Tower has been altered many times but still has many of its original features. It is the larger of the two towers that can be seen from Castle Street to the left of the main entrance.

It was strongly defended, especially on its south side, where the ten feet thick Roman masonry had been utilised to form the base and the lower part of the wall of the building. Elsewhere the walling tapers upwards to a minimum thickness of six feet.

Below ground floor level was a dungeon roughly twelve feet long by six feet wide. It had a vaulted ceiling with a maximum height of seven feet. There were no apertures for light or air and

54

The South Gate and the Barbican Tower (right).

the sole means of access was by way of the trap-door which formed the centre part of the floor above, otherwise paved with flag-stones. The room above the dungeon was a guard room and had one window.

The other room on the ground floor was of larger proportions, being about seventeen feet long by sixteen feet wide. The floor was of beaten earth and the ceiling was vaulted. Some light and ventilation was provided by a slit in the walling fifteen feet above ground level. A door, probably guarded with a portcullis, opened into the middle court, but there was no stairway then connecting the ground floor rooms to those above, of which there were three. Access to these was by way of stone stairs close to the ward wall gate.

Llewelyn the Last, had originally restricted his aggressions to North Wales, but after he extended his activities to the south

55

and had his claim to the lordship of Brecon confirmed by the King, the lord of Glamorgan was thoroughly alarmed and began to build a huge castle at Caerphilly to defend the road to Cardiff. Eventually, it was the biggest castle in Wales and in the whole of Britain, second only to Windsor Castle in the extent of the area it covered.

Construction started in 1268. When the ground work was completed after two years Llewelyn attacked and destroyed it. A new site was selected and a second attempt to build the castle was made. Again Llewelyn struck. He surrounded it and threatened the masons with starvation.

Finally, a degree of peace was restored when the King intervened and ordered both men to refrain from further aggressions. He decreed that the castle was to be held for the crown. Building operations were resumed but by the time the castle was completed, Llewelyn was dead, and the need for it no longer existed.

Other activities in Glamorgan at that time were of a very different nature. Among them was the building of the house of Greyfriars for the Franciscans which was founded either by Gilbert de Clare or by his father, Richard. The friary stood in the old suburb of Crockerton and the work of the Brotherhood there became a great influence for good among the poor at Cardiff.

When Henry III died at the age of sixty-five in 1272, having reigned ineffectually for fifty-six years, his son, Edward I, a very different character, succeeded him. Tall, handsome and resolute, he, too, was a great builder of castles. Now among the greatest tourist attractions in the country, the castles are enduring monuments to Edward, who had them built and to Llewelyn ap Gruffyd, whose activities made them necessary.

In 1282, Gilbert de Clare, divorced his wife, Alice of Angouleme, a niece of the King of France, and became affianced to Joan, King Edward's eleven year old daughter.

For Gilbert, it was a great honour to be thus closely connected to the royal house of England. For Edward, it was a very good bargain, for Gilbert received no dowry and, under the terms of the marriage settlement, was committed to agree that the Princess Joan should retain the vast Clare estates to the exclusion of Gilbert's heirs, in the very likely event that he should predecease his young wife.

Nor did his new status as son-in-law to the King give him any special privileges or favour, as became evident when he found himself in dispute with a neighbouring marcher lord, Humphrey Bohun, Earl of Hereford, who claimed ownership of the land near Merthyr, on which Gilbert had built Morlais Castle. Far from supporting him, the King found both equally guilty on charges of treason and punished them harshly.

Their estates were forfeited to the crown and they were both fined and imprisoned. Although they were subsequently released and the forfeitures deferred during their respective lifetime, their exclusive rights as marcher lords were drastically curtailed.

In 1295, Gilbert de Clare died and the Princess Joan took formal possession of his estates. Within a year, without the sanction, or indeed the knowledge of the King, she married again.

As if this was not enough she had married Ralph de Monthermer, a mere esquire, with little, if any property of his own. Her father was furious. Monthermer was arrested and imprisoned and Joan was stripped of her newly acquired possessions.

The Green Eagle on a golden shield, carried by Ralph de Monthermer.

Fortunately, for them both, the King relented and pardoned them. Monthermer was released and the Clare estates were again restored. Furthermore, Monthermer was raised to a rank befitting the son-in-law of the King. He became Earl of Hertford, Earl of Gloucester and the first lord of Glamorgan who could not trace his ancestry back to the Norman Conquest. By 1298, he had proved himself to be a great soldier, having served with distinction in the Scottish wars where he had gained victories over Robert the Bruce, himself. He was rewarded with additional estates and honours being created Earl of Atholl in Scotland and Lord of Kilkenny in Ireland.

He lost all his land and titles when his wife died in 1307, for they reverted then to her sixteen year old son by her first husband, Gilbert de Clare (III).

At the age of 68, Edward I set out on his last journey to Scotland, carried on a litter at the head of his army. The "Hammer of the Scots", as he is described on his tombstone in

Westminster Abbey, had intended to put a stop to the aggressions, once and for all, of Robert Bruce against English held castles in Scotland. He felt that Bruce was something of a traitor, since he was, like Edward, himself, of Norman origin and had been received in the English court as a friend. The King died a few miles from the border on the 7th July 1307 and strife

A view of Bute Park from inside the Keep.

and bloodshed was to continue there for many more years. Thus it was that in the same year, Edward, the Caernarvon born Prince of Wales, became King and Gilbert de Clare, his nephew, succeeded as lord of Glamorgan and was created Earl of Hertford and Earl of Gloucester.

Margaret, one of the three sisters of Gilbert, was married to Piers Gaveston. The son of a private gentleman in Gascony, he had been brought to the English court as a companion for Edward II, when he was a young boy. Although a champion jouster, being knighted by Edward I at a tournament held in honour of his son, he had developed into a most undesirable friend and was banished.

When Edward II became king, not only did he recall Gaveston, but he heaped honours upon him, creating him Baron Wallingford and Earl of Cornwall. He also appointed him Regent when he left for France to marry Isabella, the young daughter of Philip IV.

These acts of favouritism so incensed the leading barons, including Gilbert de Clare, that they took the government out of the hands of the king and appointed a group of twenty-one, the Lord Ordainers, to draw up ordinances for a new constitution. Gaveston was again banished, but when he returned Edward again treated him so well as to displease the more powerful lords. Seized by the Earl of Warwick, Gaveston was first imprisoned and then beheaded without trial in 1312.

His widow remarried. Gilbert de Clare's new brother-in-law was Hugh de Audley, who by reason of the marriage eventually succeeded him as Earl of Gloucester.

Gilbert de Clare married Maud, daughter of Richard de Burgh, Earl of Ulster in 1309. He was eighteen at that time.

Exceptionally physically strong like his father, Edward II was otherwise completely different. He was content to allow the government of the country to be in the hands of others, and had no ambition to be a soldier. He was most reluctant to go to war and did not do so until 1314, when circumstances compelled him to take military action. By then all the castles in Scotland were in Scottish hands except Stirling Castle. There, in the excepted code of medieval times, the garrison had obtained some respite by undertaking to surrender it on the 24th June if by then no help was forthcoming. The greatest army ever to cross the border prepared for battle. Near Stirling, at Bannockburn, the numerically inferior Scottish army lay in wait. They had prepared their position well.

Like the Charge of the Light Brigade in their recklessness, the heavily armoured English knights thundered in attack. Gilbert de Clare, eager for glory, led the charge.

Armour clad from the top of his helm to the girth of his charger, with sword in one hand and his shield in the other, nothing it seemed could withstand him.

But hidden in the grass were the caltraps. The small but deadly weapons proved decisive. The horses screamed with pain, lamed by the viscious iron spikes that had been thrown in their path. They reared and threw their riders. Many fell, impaled on the sharpened stakes in the turf covered pits prepared for them. It was not a battle; it was a massacre. The knights were slaughtered as they lay helpless. Among the first to die, was Gilbert de Clare, the third and last of the lords of Glamorgan to bear that name.

Clare blood was spilled that day at Bannockburn. It continued to flow, however, in the veins of the victor, for Robert Bruce, himself, was a descendant of the first Gilbert de Clare lord of Cardiff Castle.

Another to fight at Bannockburn was Ralph de Monthermer, step-father of the Gilbert who was slain. He was more fortunate. He survived, and although captured, was released by Bruce, who remembered him with gratitude as one who had befriended him in the court of Edward I many years before.

It says much for the personality of the man who started life as a mere esquire and later became a knight celebrated for his campaigns against the Scots, that he should be welcome in Scotland where he took for his second wife one of greatest of the Scottish heiresses. He married Isabel, widow of John de Hastings, and sister and co-heiresses of Aymer de Valence, Earl of Pembroke. Her late husband, like the father of Bruce, himself, and John Balliol, who was briefly King of Scotland, had been among the more important of the claimants to the Scottish throne following the death of Alexander III.

When, many years later, the granddaughter of Ralph de Monthermer and Princess Joan married Sir John de Montacute, the arms of the two families were combined. The famous green eagle on the gold field of Monthermer and the three silver fusils, or elongated diamonds, on the red background of Montacute were quartered, forming one shield. In consequence, the banner of the low-born Monthermer, with that of the ancient Montagu family, can be seen proudly flying over stately homes even today.

CHAPTER SEVEN

The Despensers, The Supreme Royalists

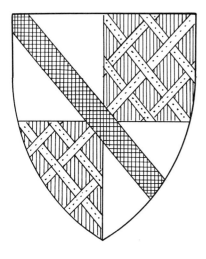

The Despenser Arms. This is the only shield depicted upside down at Cardiff Castle, the sign of armorial degradation. Sir Hugh le Despenser was compelled to wear his coat armour when he was hung, drawn and quartered in 1326.

When Gilbert de Clare was slain, still only twenty-two years old, his widow claimed that she was pregnant. Two years passed and no child was born. The Clare estates were then divided and settled upon his three sisters, all young, but all married.

Meanwhile, the lordship of Glamorgan was held in ward by the crown and it was during this period that Llewelyn Bren, lord of Senghennydd, rebelled and brought terror again to South Wales.

He was captured and imprisoned in the Tower of London. Eventually, the king pardoned and released him. On his return to Glamorgan, however, he was seized and despite the King's pardon, was executed in the most barbaric fashion.

As part of her share of the Clare estates, Gilbert's sister, Eleanor, took possession of Cardiff Castle and her husband became in 1317 the first of the four members of his family to be lords of Glamorgan.

He was Sir Hugh le Despenser, who, like his late brother-in-law, Piers Gaveston, had been knighted by Edward I. Indeed, the two of them, together with Edward II, then Prince of Wales, had received the Accolade on the same Easter Day at the grand tournament arranged by the King in honour of his son. He had been made governor of Odiham Castle, had accompanied the King on his expedition to Gascony and had, two years later, fought at the English victory at Dunbar in Scotland. He had also been appointed to negotiate peace treaties with the kings of the Romans and the French and to visit the papal court as ambassador.

The name "Le Despenser" was derived from the office of steward held by an ancestor, Robert, in the household of

The Ladies Walk.

William the Conqueror. Other members of the family had subsequently held the same post under later kings.

The family motto, "Pro Magna Carta," proudly proclaimed that the Despensers were in favour of upholding the Great Charter, which another ancestor had helped to bring into being. He had been one of the group of barons at Runnymede, who had compelled King John to agree to irs provisions.

Yet another ancestor had been Justiciar of England in the reign of Henry III. He had been killed, like Simon de Montfort, at the Battle of Evesham.

The new lord of Glamorgan was the son of the Earl of Winchester, also called Hugh le Despenser and of Isabel, daughter of William Beauchamp, Earl of Warwick. Her brother Guy, was the Earl of Warwick concerned in the execution of Piers Gaveston, the favourite of Edward II. Hugh le Despenser was destined to succeed Gaveston in the affection of that weak king.

By 1321, Hugh le Despenser and his father, too, had become

63

as detested by other great lords as Gaveston had been. With the King's concurrence, they had become virtually the rulers of the country and immensely rich in the process. This was particularly the case in Glamorgan and South Wales generally, where other marcher lords, including the husbands of his wife's co-heiresses considered that the lord of Glamorgan was using his influence with the King to cheat them of their lands..

There was a great outcry, that threatened to develop into another rebellion, concerning the Llewelyn Bren atrocity. An enquiry into it was ordered. It resulted in Hugh le Despenser having Sir William Fleming, Lord of Wenvoe, his sheriff at Cardiff Castle, executed on a gibbet raised outside the Black Tower. Some historians state that Sir William Fleming was merely a scape-goat, and that he had carried out the orders of Hugh le Despenser, himself, when he had wrongfully put the Welsh lord to death.

The turning point in the careers of the Despenser father and son came when Queen Isabella, since known as the "She Wolf of France," having been to France, ostensibly to negotiate on behalf of her husband with her brother, Charles IV of France, returned to England, accompanied by her lover, Roger Mortimer, and a mercenary army. Joined by other disgruntled barons she made war on the King and the Despensers.

Finding no support in England, they hurried to Wales and, making the great castle at Caerphilly their headquarters, summoned those who owed them allegiance in Glamorgan. Few answered the call. In desperation the King appealed to the Queen, but in vain. No reconciliation was effected. He fled but was eventually captured by her troops in a wood near Llantrisant. Both the Despensers were taken, the younger, believed to have been making his way to the Isle of Lundy, was trapped in the Garth Mountains.

In 1327, a Parliament met at Westminster. None but the King's enemies attended. Under pressure from Isabella and Mortimer, Edward II was compelled to sign a document acknowledging his mis-rule and abdicating. For a time he was imprisoned in a filthy dungeon in a state of near starvation. Then, after eight months of this treatment had failed to kill him, he was murdered in Berkeley Castle.

The Despensers were executed. The elder, the Earl of

Stained glass portrait of Eleanor de Clare.

Winchester, was beheaded at Gloucester, having first been hanged on a gallows in sight of Edward II, who was at that time a prisoner, and of his young son, later to become Edward III. His body was cut up and fed to the dogs and his head taken and exhibited in his earldom at Winchester,

Hugh, the younger, was impeached before Parliament. He was sentenced "to be drawn upon a hurdle, with trumps and trumpets, throughout all the city of Hereford, and being there hanged and quartered." This sentence was executed on a gallows fifty feet high.

Thus ended the career of the first lord of Glamorgan not to hold the Earldom of Gloucester. Since he, like his father, had been sentenced to armorial degradation, he was compelled to don his coat armour before execution. In those days of chivalry, that was considered to be the supreme humiliation. It is for this reason that the shield of Hugh le Despenser, alone, of all those of the lords of Glamorgan, depicted in stained-glass around the Banqueting Hall at Cardiff Castle, is shown upside down. It is the traditional way of illustrating knightly dishonour.

After the execution of Hugh le Despenser in November, 1326, Eleanor, his widow, and children were imprisoned in the Tower of London, where they remained until the following February.

Two years later, she married William la Zouche of Mortimer, constable of the Tower of London, who had led the party that captured her first husband.

Despite the fact that the marriage had taken place without the consent of the young King Edward III, she was placed in possession of her share of the Clare estates and William la Zouche became, through her, lord of Glamorgan, and the new master of Cardiff Castle. She did not, however, have any control of her late husband's own property. It is interesting to see how he had prospered as favourite of Edward II and how sharing with his father, such unprecedented power within the government of the country, had brought him wealth, which in present day terms is difficult to estimate.

His wife's share of the Clare estates in 1317 consisted of land extending from Cardiff to Neath, together with castles and other buildings and property, which was valued in money terms at that time at £1,276 6s. 9¾d. What the property would

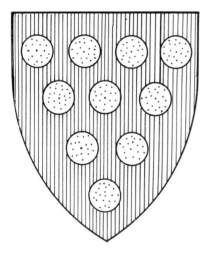

Ten Besants of gold on a red shield. The Arms of William la Zouche.

Hugh le Despenser II.

worth in the deflated currency of today is impossible to calculate. Yet it is as nothing compared with his wealth at the time of his execution. In a petition presented by his grandson for restitution it is detailed as follows:—

Elizabeth de Montacute.

59 lordships in various parts of the country, 28,000 sheep, 1,000 oxen, 1,200 cows and their calves, 2,000 pigs, 3,000 bullocks, 40 mares with their colts, 1,600 draught horses on farms, 40 tuns of wine, 10 tuns of cider in a number of butteries, 600 sides of bacon, 80 carcases of beef, and 600 of lamb in larders. He also possessed armour plate, jewels and ready money with various bankers to a value of £10,000, 36 sacks of wool, and a library of books.

William la Zouche became justice of all the royal forests, south of the Trent. He had a son, Alan, by his previous wife, widow of Guy de Beauchamp Earl of Warwick, and another, Hugh, by Eleanor. Neither had any rights in the Despenser estates.

Eleanor died in 1337 and her son by her first marriage, Hugh le Despenser (II) succeeded as Lord of Glamorgan. He served in both the Scottish wars and in France. He married Elizabeth, widow of Giles de Baddlesmere, and daughter of John de Montacute.

As soon as he was able, Edward III firmly took the reigns of government into his own hands and avenged the murder of his father. Mortimer was executed and the faithless queen, Isabella was banished from the court by her son. She ended her days in a convent.

As the son of Isabella, and the grandson of Philip IV, with some justification, Edward claimed the throne of France. He spent most of his life trying to enforce by arms the right to rule that mere assertion failed to establish.

He had many successes, but his most famous victory, the Battle of Cressy, might well have been a devastating defeat, had it not been for the valour and leadership of the second Hugh le Despenser, lord of Glamorgan.

Edward's army had swept aside all resistance in Normandy, but the advance to the northern ports was hampered by the widespread destruction of the river bridges. Short of food and supplies, the adverse conditions began to affect morale. Then, when all seemed lost, Hugh le Despenser found a ford and led the way across the River Somme. His small party of Welsh long-bowmen followed him, bows held aloft. Safely on the other side with bowstrings still dry, they succeeded in holding off 3,000 Frenchmen until their weary, sick and near starving companions crossed, and established themselves and took up a defensible position. There, a French army vastly superior in numbers and arms was defeated.

Edward le Despenser.

The lord of Glamorgan died in 1349, a victim of the terrible Black Death which swept across Europe. In England it struck down one person in three. He was buried at Tewkesbury at the abbey where the choir, the ambulatory and the vaulting were almost completely rebuilt by the munificence of his widow.

Over his tomb she had his effigy in alabaster, as a knight in armour, placed, in the magnificent Despenser chantry.

Hugh le Despenser died childless, so it was his nephew, Edward, who succeeded him at Cardiff Castle in 1349. It was recorded at that time that Cardiff was a walled town. Although it is not known when the transformation was completed, it seems certain that it was a gradual process commencing, probably, at the time of the Llewelyn Bren uprising that resulted in the old defences of ditch, earthen banking and wooden palisades being replaced by walls of stone.

Edward le Despenser was another famous soldier. Still in his teens, he had accompanied the Black Prince on his campaigns and was with the King's son at the Battle of Poitiers in 1356 when the French were defeated and their king, Jean, captured.

In the highest tradition of that age of chivalry, Jean was treated with the courtesy befitting his rank and the Black Prince, himself, waited upon him at table. Nevertheless, he was taken captive to England, where he was an honoured prisoner for many years. Another royal captive in England, at that time, was Robert Bruce's son, David II, of Scotland. He had been captured at the Battle of Nevill's Cross.

King Jean was released in 1360, after part of the huge ransom demanded had been paid and hostages given to guarantee payment of the balance. Jean's son, the Duke of Anjou, one of the hostages, outraged his father's sense of honour by breaking his parole and escaping. Thereupon, King Jean voluntarily returned to captivity, and still a prisoner, died in England in 1364.

Edward III, obsessed by the legends of King Arthur, created his own order of knighthood. Restricted to twenty-six members, including the King himself, and his son, it became and remains today, the most exclusive in the world. Its origin is obscure, but is believed to have been formed to provide two teams of the most noble and expert knights for jousting at the royal tournaments. Its symbol was the Garter.

Among the first to be installed in the Order, in recognition of his gallantry, was Edward le Despenser. He married Elizabeth, the daughter of another Garter Knight, Bartholomew, Baron Burghersh. They had two sons and four daughters.

When Edward le Despenser died, in 1375, he, too, was interred at Tewkesbury. His effigy, as a kneeling figure on the roof of the Trinity Chantry, is probably unique. Most knights are shown in a reclining position.

His elder son, Thomas, succeeded him and was at first known as Lord Despenser of Glamorgan. He married Constance, daughter of Edmund Plantagent, Duke of York, the fifth son of Edward III.

Thomas le Despenser accompanied Richard II on his expedition to Ireland in 1395 and remained a close companion of that monarch. They had much in common. Both had lost their fathers at an early age, victims of the Black Death; Richard's father, the Black Prince, had died in 1377, ten years after the birth of his son, and since Thomas le Despenser was born in 1373, he was only two when his father died.

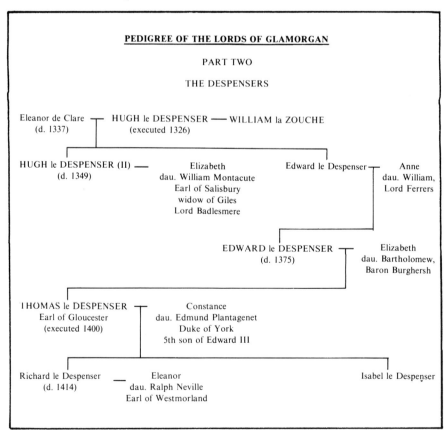

PEDIGREE OF THE LORDS OF GLAMORGAN

PART TWO

THE DESPENSERS

Eleanor de Clare ――― HUGH le DESPENSER ――― WILLIAM la ZOUCHE
(d. 1337)   (executed 1326)

HUGH le DESPENSER (II) ―――   Elizabeth   Edward le Despenser ― Anne
(d. 1349)   dau. William Montacute   dau. William,
                         Earl of Salisbury   Lord Ferrers
                         widow of Giles
                         Lord Badlesmere

                                    EDWARD le DESPENSER ― Elizabeth
                                         (d. 1375)   dau. Bartholomew,
                                                            Baron Burghersh

THOMAS le DESPENSER ―   Constance
Earl of Gloucester   dau. Edmund Plantagenet
(executed 1400)   Duke of York
                            5th son of Edward III

Richard le Despenser ――   Eleanor   Isabel le Despenser
(d. 1414)   dau. Ralph Neville
                            Earl of Westmorland

In 1398, Richard reversed the sentence of banishment that had been passed by Parliament against Thomas's great-grandfather, Hugh le Despenser, and consequently Thomas le Despenser was created Earl of Gloucester by reason of his descent from the Clare Earls of Gloucester through Hugh's wife Eleanor.

By 1399, King Richard had been deposed by his cousin, Bolingbroke, who usurped the throne as Henry IV. It was then enough that Thomas le Despenser was the husband of Richard's cousin, to ensure that he, the last Despenser lord of Glamorgan in the male line, should die, as the first one had done, by execution.

Suspected of plotting to restore Richard to the throne, he was seized in Bristol and taken by the rabble to the market place. There, he was beheaded in the street.

Among his fellow lords of Glamorgan, he is shown in stained-glass at Cardiff Castle with a sword poised over his head. It symbolises the manner of his death.

Introduction to the Fifteenth Century

Changes in the relationship between the English and the Welsh had drastically altered with the death of the last Llewelyn. Edward I had been determined and ruthless in establishing and maintaining order in both England and in Wales but he had been wise enough to realise that he would have to rely on the good will of the Welsh and their leaders if a state of peace was to be preserved.

Consequently, more and more of the administration of their country was placed in Welsh hands.

Although the marcher lordship system of defence was retained in some areas, many of the lordships came under the direct control of the crown. The old Welsh shires of Anglesey, Caernarvon, Merioneth, Cardigan and Carmarthen, became the Principality, the responsibility of the Prince of Wales, from that time, traditionally, the eldest son of the reigning monarch.

That meant that there were three different and distinct types of government in Wales.

There was local rule in the marches by individual lords, some of them Welsh, a wider, more compact, area controlled by the Prince of Wales without representation in the English parliament, and the crown lands, which were administered in the same way as the English counties.

A sign of changing times, was the writ to Morgan ap Meredith for service in Gascony. It was probably the first issued directly to any Welshman by an English king. The day of general enlistment was approaching.

Other significant acts were appointments of Welshmen to defend such strategic areas as the port of Kenfig, which was

74

done shortly after Morgan of Afan had been committed to the Tower of London in 1314.

The making of other proclamations protecting the Welsh in the courts was significant, too. It was decreed, for example, that disputes between Welsh parties should be decided under Welsh law, and where both English and Welsh litigants were involved, such cases should be decided upon by a jury half Welsh and half English.

An enquiry regarding local custom, "Placita de quo warranto", was put in hand to preserve common law usage and this led to the giving of sanctions to live by established local customs in Wales, as elsewhere. This right was enforceable under royal authority.

Unhappily, the steady progress towards harmonious integration of the two nations was interrupted during the weak rule of Edward II. The unjust and cruel execution of Llewelyn Bren led to unrest which developed into warfare.

The lordship of Glamorgan was attacked by rival marcher lords supported by their Welsh allies. Both the royal authority and that of the lord of Glamorgan within his lordship was defied. When writs were issued for enlistment to resist the mercenary forces of Edward's French-born queen, they were ignored and the king was left without a significant fighting force.

It is interesting to note that of those selected by Edward to appeal for peace, one was a Welshman, Rhys ap Griffiths, the Abbot of Neath. Unfortunately for the king the eloquence of the Abbot failed to move Queen Isabella and Roger Mortimer.

The murder of Edward II, the preoccupation of Edward III in Continental wars, the early death of the Black Prince, the Black Death which reduced the population to a point where there were insufficient labourers to produce enough food, all had serious consequences for the well-being of the people of both countries.

There was, however, a growing awareness of a common interest between the two nations. Many Welshmen had served with English comrades both in Scotland and in France. They had learned to appreciate the fighting qualities of each other. The Welsh long-bowman, in particular, had gained recognition for what he undoubtedly was, the finest and the most deadly archer in Europe.

More and more Welshmen came to England for their education, especially those of the old princely families. They were appointed to high office in their own country, although in the changing political atmosphere then prevailing, some became impatient when promotion appeared to them to be slow, and envious of Englishmen already established in positions of trust.

Such a man was Owen Glendower. He owned land in Cardiganshire and was a blood relative of princely families in both north and south Wales. He was educated in the Inns of Court in London and in the household of Henry Bolingbroke, becoming a squire and a soldier skilled in medieval warfare.

He took part in tournaments and fought in the Scottish wars and probably in Ireland and France as well. He married a lady, whose family, long resident in Wales were of English origin. He seemed eager for and set on a course likely to win high office under the English crown. Then, following a dispute with an English rival, Henry Grey, over the ownership of land situated between their neighbouring estates, Glendower changed direction when Bolingbroke, his former patron, became king as Henry IV, after the deposition and probable murder of Richard II.

He was an imposing figure, tall and strong. Trained in the finest medieval school of warfare, with the knowledge of, and the ability and ruthlessness to use the latest engines and siege weapons, with supporters everywhere in Wales, even in the ranks of the castle defenders, he brought terror, destruction and death to the land. With local knowledge of terrain, he was able to travel far and fast in weather conditions which immobilised the English forces. It is little wonder that, even during his lifetime he became a legendary figure; a devil incarnate to the English, but a demi-god to the Welsh.

CHAPTER EIGHT

The Beauchamps and the Nevilles

In 1404, Owen Glendower attacked Cardiff Castle. The lordship of Glamorgan was again in ward at that time, since Thomas le Despenser, whose Barony of Despenser and Earldom of Gloucester had fallen under attainder after his execution, had left only an infant son, Richard. A daughter, Isabel, was born posthumously.

The attack was part of Glendower's campaign of armed aggression in defiance of King Henry IV, who was still regarded by many, especially in Wales, as the usurper of the throne of Richard II.

After that unfortunate king had died, apparently by starvation, a prisoner in Pontefract Castle, the Welsh Prince, once Henry's friend, became his implaccable foe. So successful was he, that the superstitious and baffled English army, fighting in unfamiliar country, accredited him with supernatural powers. They began to believe that he could command the elements; that storm and deluge, mist and rain, thunder and lightning, all obeyed him.

Glendower besieged the castle, breached its walls and forced an entrance putting its defenders to the sword. He spared nothing. The town, too, was burned, houses, churches and other buildings. One street alone survived, the street of the Greyfriars convent. This was spared out of reverence for the Franciscan Brotherhood, yet even they suffered as a result of the Glendower visitation, for fearing to lose their treasures and records they had taken them to the castle which they, in common with everybody else, believed to be impregnable.

Richard le Despenser married Elizabeth, the daughter of Ralph Neville, Earl of Westmorland, but died childless in 1414.

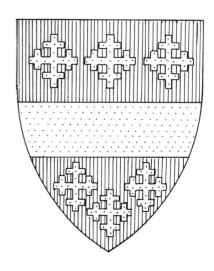

A fess and six Cross-crosslets in gold and red. The Beauchamp Arms.
'Fortuna mea in bello campo'.
(My lot is in fair ground).

Richard's sister, Isabel le Despenser, at the age of eleven, had married three years earlier. Her husband, Richard Beauchamp, Earl of Worcester, through her, became lord of Glamorgan.

Worcester's cousin, was also called Richard Beauchamp. He was one of the most celebrated soldiers of his age. A Knight of the Bath at the time of the coronation of Henry IV, he distinguished himself both against Glendower and the Welsh Prince's northern ally, Henry Percy, Earl of Northumberland, the famous, "Harry Hotspur." He was then honoured with the Garter.

When Henry of Monmouth, became Henry V, Warwick was appointed Lord High Steward of England for the coronation.

He was of the "Few, the happy few, the band of brothers" who fought with Henry at Agincourt. He was present, too, when the King married in Paris in 1420.

Two years later, the Earl of Worcester, the lord of Glamorgan, died. He fell, mortally wounded at the siege of Meaux. Isabel had her husband interred in a new chantry at Tewkesbury, the Beauchamp Chantry, where in due course she, too, was laid at rest.

In the winter of 1421, Catherine, daughter of Charles VI of France gave birth to a son at Windsor. On 31st August, 1422, the father, Henry V of England died at Vincennes. Shortly afterwards, the grandfather, Charles VI died, too. So Henry VI, a child, less than one year old became the acknowledged king of France in the north and east of that country as well as the undoubted king of England. His was to be one of the longest reigns and one of the most disastrous in history.

In 1423, Isabel le Despenser re-married. Her second husband, was Richard Beauchamp, Earl of Warwick, her first husband's cousin. She was still only twenty one years of age at the time.

The new lord of Glamorgan took possession of a Cardiff Castle, which like the town of Cardiff, itself, was still in a ruinous condition as a result of the Glendower revolt.

Nobody knew what had become of the great rebel. He had just disappeared, and nobody was ever to know, or where, he died. Like King Arthur, Glendower just faded away.

Richard Beauchamp, Earl of Warwick, put in hand work,

which according to a Charter granted in 1451 by Beauchamp's son-in-law, Richard Neville, resulted in Cardiff being completely refortified with walls, tower-gates and ditches.

He also repaired and strengthened the Castle defences. Not only was the Black Tower restored, but alterations were made

The Octagonal Tower.

to the Residential Tower in the Keep where bigger windows were introduced. Most of all, he built the Beauchamp Tower.

The building of the great new Octagonal Tower along the outer side of the west wall of the castle was a development of the greatest significance in the history of Cardiff Castle.

Although the new tower with its battlements and arrow slits was intended solely as an additional defence to the reconstructed West Gate of the town, which was situated immediately below it, from it grew the complex of buildings making up the Cardiff Castle of today.

Sometime between 1425 and 1439, a Great Hall was built along the inner side of the wall. The passages, cut through the thickness of the wall, originally used to afford a means of access to the Beauchamp Tower from the inner court of the bailey, were utilised to connect the Tower with the Great Hall.

Up to that time, the lords of Glamorgan, had lived in buildings, either in the Bailey or the Keep of the Castle. In the more settled times of the Beauchamps, they were able to move into the much more comfortable lodgings that the Great Hall provided.

The Octagonal Tower extended approximately twenty feet beyond and along the outside of the wall and the Great Hall, about seventy feet long, protruded into the inner court some twenty three feet.

When William shared out the spoils after the Conquest, he gave each of his companions in arms a number of small landed estates widely separated one from the other throughout the country. In this way he ensured that no one lord, or indeed any small group of them, could concentrate enough power in any area sufficient to challenge his supremacy.

Slowly over a period of many generations, by exploiting the Norman laws of succession and by carefully arranging marriages, a number of families succeeded in becoming a threat to the crown. Two such families were the Beauchamps and the Nevilles.

Richard Beauchamp was a great landowner even before he married Isabel Despenser. He had estates in England and in Wales. Richard Neville, Earl of Salisbury, was another. He was a descendant of John of Gaunt, Duke of Lancaster, the immensely rich younger son of Edward III.

A silver saltire on red. The Neville Arms.
'Ne vile' (Not vile)
or
'Ne vile valis'
(Form no vile wish).

The mottoes of both the Beauchamps and the Nevilles are allusive, being examples of the Medieval practice of basing mottoes on puns of the names.

Both fought in France and shared in the victory at Agincourt. They were together, too, at the disastrous siege of Orleans, where Joan of Arc inspired her countrymen, and present, later, at her trial and execution, when she was burnt at at the stake as a witch.

Richard Beauchamp had two children, Henry and Anne. Marriages were arranged for both of them with the children of Richard Neville. Henry, when only ten years old was married to Cecily Neville. His sister, Anne, married Richard Neville, junior. Since the bridegrooms were the heirs of their families' fortunes, it was highly probable that ultimately, the two huge estates would be combined. This, in fact, happened.

The lord of Glamorgan and his wife Isabel, both died in 1439, and their son, Henry Beauchamp, succeeded to the lordship and to the Earldom of Warwick.

Henry Beauchamp, like his father, was a soldier, and within two years of his father's death, although he was not, at that time, nineteen years of age, he tendered his service for the defence of Acquitaine.

His prestige in France was immense for he was the son of the man who had been, not only appointed by the will of Henry V as the governor of his baby son, but who had also become Lieutenant-General of the whole Realm of France and Duchy of Normandy.

The twenty-two year old king, Henry VI heaped honours upon Henry Beauchamp. He created him Premier Earl of England and granted him, and his heirs, the right to wear a golden coronet about his head, even in the presence of the king. Three days later he advanced him to the rank of duke with precedence over all other with the exception only of the Duke of Norfolk.

This last honour so displeased the Duke of Buckingham that another act of Parliament was passed to molify him to some degree declaring that the Dukes of Warwick and of Buckingham should have seniority, one over the other, alternatively, for periods of one year.

Warwick was granted additional estates, too. These included the Channel Islands. Then, just before he died in 1445, still only twenty-two years old, he was crowned, King of the Isle of Wight, by Henry VI, himself.

When Henry Beauchamp died, his dukedom expired, too, but his other honours devolved upon his two-year old daughter, Anne, Countess of Warwick, who became ward of Queen Margaret.

At the age of six, the young Countess died, too, and then the Warwick estates passed to her aunt and namesake, the wife of Richard Neville, who himself became Earl of Warwick, lord of Glamorgan and master of Cardiff Castle.

Since his father, the Earl of Westmorland had married Alice, daughter and heiress fo Thomas, Earl of Salisbury and holder of the baronies of Montacute and Monthermer, in the course of time, Richard Neville succeeded to all these honours. He is better known, however, as "Warwick the Kingmaker." He has been described as, "the greatest and last of the old Norman chivalry-knight, kinglier in pride, in state, in possessions and in renown than the king, himself."

At the beginning of the Wars of the Roses he used his great resources in support of the House of York. He fought at the first Battle of St. Albans, at Northampton, at Wakefield and again at St. Albans. He then proclaimed the young Earl of March in

The West Gate, the Gate House of which was restored in 1451.

Isabel Neville.

London as King Edward IV and by his victory at Towton Field
set him firmly on the throne.

A few years, later, however, discontented with Edward's rule,
he unseated him and restored his Lancastrian rival, Henry VI,
but, as the old king had become an imbecile, Warwick, himself,
was master of England.

Richard Neville had two daughters, Isabel and Anne. Isabel he married to George, Duke of Clarence, brother of Edward IV, when he and Clarence formed an alliance to overthrow Edward. Anne he wed to Edward, the young Prince of Wales, when he became reconciled to Queen Margaret and determined to restore King Henry. Thus, one of Warwick's daughters was married to the brother of the Yorkist King and the other to the son-and-heir of the Lancastrian Monarch.

The Kingmaker's last battle was fought at Barnet on Easter Day 1471. In dense fog and in utter confusion, his retainers slaughtered each other, unable to distinguish friend from foe. Warwick, himself, was slain and Edward regained the throne. Henry VI died, apparently murdered in the Tower of London and Edward, the Prince of Wales, was already dead, killed at, or executed after, the Battle of Tewkesbury.

CHAPTER NINE

The Plantagenets

George Plantagenet, had been created Duke of Clarence in 1461, when his brother first became King as Edward IV. The title of Clarence was derived from the honour of Clare, the seat of the early lords of Glamorgan.

It was apt, therefore, if surprising, in view of Clarence's treachery to his brother in alliance with Warwick, that after the Kingmaker was slain, he was advanced by letters patent to the earldoms of Warwick and Salisbury, and as husband of Isabel Neville, becoming through her, lord of Glamorgan.

This did not please his younger brother, Richard, Duke of Gloucester, who had married Isabel's sister, Anne, the widow of Edward, Prince of Wales. He considered, with some reason, that his wife, co-heiress of her father, was entitled to her share of the Beauchamp and Neville estates.

Even less did it please Warwick's widow, Anne Beauchamp, the true heiress and the mother of Isabel and Anne, who had been disinherited by the Act of Edward IV, which allowed her estates to be distributed as if she were already dead. She was destined to spend the rest of her life, not as the richest woman in the kingdom, as she was entitled to expect, but in abject poverty.

Since his brother the King, had so graciously forgiven him for his treachery in 1469, it is surprising that nine years later, Clarence should have been accused and convicted on charges of treason for which the penalty was death. He spent some time in the Tower of London, where he died, secretly, it is said, drowned in a butt of malmsey.

As Clarence had established his right to the Lordship of Glamorgan, his son, Edward, Duke of Warwick, should have succeeded him. Instead, his uncle, Richard, Duke of Gloucester, became the next Lord of Glamorgan, and the luckless Warwick, merely because he was the son of his father, was kept under restraint for the rest of his life.

While resident in the Castle, Richard's wife, Anne Neville,

George, Duke of Clarence.

King Richard III.

played an active part in the life of Cardiff. She paid for the beautiful tower, the work of Hart, added to the parish church of St. John the Baptist. It is probable, that this reconstruction had been commissioned originally by her sister, Isabel.

After the death of his brother, Edward IV, and his uncrowned nephew, Edward V, the Duke of Gloucester became king as Richard III, and the lordship of Glamorgan was merged in the crown.

The circumstances of his accession to the throne have been the subject of many stories, most of them biased.

Shakespeare with his huge readership has shown him as a monster, and consequently millions of people all over the world believe that he was. Nevertheless, a playwright depending on royal patronage in Tudor times was hardly likely to show the last of the Plantagenets in the most favourable light. Richard may have murdered the imbecile king Henry VI, the young Prince of Wales, Edward, and the even younger Princes in the Tower, his own nephews, or he may have been, as some now believe, the most maligned king in history.

What made the Wars of the Roses so horrifying was the abandonment of the code of chivalry of earlier times. A vanquished foe received no mercy. Both sides were equally guilty of executing prisoners in cold blood. The result was that few of the great and ancient families excaped extinction including the Plantagenets, themselves. So numerous at the beginning of the Wars, when Richard III, became king, only one other of their number in the male line was still alive. He was Richard's nephew, Clarence's son, Edward, Earl of Warwick and he was a prisoner in the castle at Sheriff-Hutton in Yorkshire.

CHAPTER TEN

The Coming of the Herberts

During the three score years and ten that had elapsed since the Glendower campaigns, England had become impoverished by wars abroad and by power struggles at home.

The triumphs of Henry V had been succeeded by disasters in France and the suicidal rivalries of the last of the Plantagenets.

Although relatively few people had been involved personally, in the Wars of the Roses, which were essentially tournaments of the grand scale fought by armour-clad knights supported by their private armies of retainers, the English were weary of conflict and longed for peace. They cared less for the niceties of royal succession than of the abilities of their rulers to maintain a peaceful and an ordered society.

Cardiff had long remained in ruins after the visitation of Owen Glendower, but had emerged at last repaired and rebuilt by the Earl of Warwick, who had also done much work on the devastated castle, including construction work along the west wall. This became and still is the centre piece of the modern castle buildings.

The spirit of the Welsh people was at a low ebb, but was being heartened by the poets who promised them a new messiah and a brighter future.

It was then that Henry Tudor landed in the Little England beyond Wales, as Pembroke is called, and sought the Welsh support of his uncle, Jasper Tudor. He then marched on to win the crown at the battle of Bosworth in 1485.

His triumph was greeted with joy throughout Wales and although disillusionment was to succeed the initial rapture as it became evident that the first of the Tudor monarchs was to be too busy in establishing his rule in England to do much for the

Jasper Tudor.

Katherine Woodville, wife of Jasper
Tudor.

betterment of the Welsh, it was some consolation to them to know that at last a Welsh king ruled in England.

Although it is probable that Henry VII understood Welsh, his son Henry VIII did not. Nor would he be willing to rely on interpreters. It is not surprising therefore that when the Acts of 1536 and 1542 were drafted in order to do what centuries of bloodshed had failed to achieve, they included clauses that were not welcomed by the Welsh.

The Acts did not actively discourage the speaking of the Welsh tongue, but they did make a knowledge of English an advantage. This was because it became a condition for attaining high office under the crown. It was rather like the adoption of the metric system by the British as a condition to entry to the Common market. Neither were popular measures but had obvious practical advantages for it is easier and less time consuming for a small minority to accept the language or system of the majority.

The reign of Henry VIII was a time of drastic and fundamental change. Many systems and institutions had outgrown their usefulness. This was particularly so in Wales where, small though it was in area and the population few in numbers, the Crown Lands, the Principality and the marcher lordships, each had a different type of administration.

Like the monastries that had served mankind so well in earlier times, the marcher lordships, the buffer states between two warring nations, no longer had a useful role to play when old antagonists became one people under a common king. Indeed, the lordships had become a menace to peace for they provided a "No Go" area capable of giving sanctuary to predators, who like the wicked barons in King Stephen's troubled reign, could rest secure within a stronghold between raids, on the property of the law abiding citizens outside.

Both monastries and lordships were abolished. Although their lords were allowed to retain their lands, they were stripped of their personal power and special privileges.

It was in those days of radical change that a family long resident in Wales became lords of Cardiff and the ancient castle. Although the lordships were absorbed into the new shires, then created, and given parliamentary representation in common with the English counties, by the unique charter of Henry's son,

Edward VI, the Herberts, alone, were enabled to exercise many of the powers of the marcher lords.

Traditionally, a remote ancestor of theirs was chamberlain in the Court of William Rufus and, as such, would have been well acquainted with the first Norman lord of Glamorgan, Robert Fitzhamon.

An even remoter ancestor is said to have been the Great Charlemagne, Emperor of the West from A.D. 800 to A.D. 814. Such claims, however, are difficult to prove.

Of undoubted authenticity, however, was their connection with Sir William Herbert, the first Earl of Pembroke of a creation earlier than theirs, of Raglan Castle. He was one of the

Henry VII.

93

most active participants on the Yorkist side of the conflict in the Wars of the Roses. He was the grandson of his namesake, who became the lord of Cardiff Castle.

Introduction to the Tudor Period

After the death of Henry V in 1422 his widow, Catherine of France, married Owen Tudor and they had two sons, Edmund and Jasper. Henry VI, their half-brother, created them, respectively, Earl of Richmond and Earl of Pembroke.

Owen, Edmund and Jasper, were all active Lancastrians and during the Wars of the Roses, Owen and Edmund were both killed. Jasper was more fortunate. He escaped and went into exile, taking Henry Tudor, Edmund's young son, born post-humously to Margaret Beaufort, daughter of the Duke of Somerset, with him.

In 1485 Henry, then twenty-seven years old, returned, accompanied by his uncle Jasper and landed at Milford Haven. There they were joined by other powerful lords dissatisfied with Richard's rule. A battle was fought at Bosworth Field on 22nd August and Richard was defeated and killed. His body was taken and buried in a remote monastry in Leicestershire.

With the death of the last Plantagenet king, the first lord of Glamorgan to have ascended the throne, both the crown and the lordship passed to Henry VII, the first of the Tudor monarchs.

In gratitude to his uncle, the only father figure he had ever known, Henry created Jasper Tudor, Duke of Bedford at the Tower of London on 27th October, 1485. His Grace, a privy councillor, Justice of South Wales, and Lord-Lieutenant of Ireland was invested with the Garter. Furthermore, he became Lord of Glamorgan and of Cardiff Castle.

He it was, who added the four bays to the front of Richard Beauchamp's Great Hall that are still a notable feature to the castle lodgings along the west wall of Cardiff Castle. He is believed, too, to have made certain alterations to the Keep where bigger windows were introduced.

In 1486, Anne Beauchamp, Countess of Warwick, who had out lived both of her daughters, petitioned for the repeal of the Act of Edward IV by which she had been deprived of her inheritance. This was granted, but since she immediately entered into a Deed re-granting the lordship to the king, who promptly re-instated Jasper Tudor, it would appear that the purpose of the exercise was merely to regularise the situation on a legal basis and had no practical effect so far as the unfortunate Countess was concerned.

Jasper died in 1495, when under another Act of Parliament, the lordship passed to the King's second son, the future Henry VIII, who, notwithstanding the Act, appears to have exercised no authority in the lordship during the lifetime of his father.

The era of the marcher lords virtually ended with the coming of the Tudors. Many of their families had been wiped out during the Wars of the Roses and their lordships had been merged with the crown. Of the remainder, since there was no longer a need for them, they were doomed. They had been established to keep order in the border country, but with a king on the throne proud to call himself a Welshman, despite having also French and English blood in his veins, the union of Wales with England had at long last come to be an accepted fact.

Just as he took the roses of the warring Lancastrians and Yorkists, and combined them to form the Tudor rose of peace, so he adopted the Red Dragon symbol. He fought under it at Bosworth and he incorporated it in his royal arms. In doing so, he sought to foster the idea that he was King Arthur, the fabulous, returned to deliver his people.

He had his first-born son christened Arthur, too, and ensured, as far as he was able, that he should rule one day. Just as Richard III had removed a rival to the throne, so did the first Tudor king.

Since Edward, Earl of Warwick, the son of Clarence, was the true heir, and should, according to established rules of succession, have been king of England as well as lord of Glamorgan, Henry had him transferred to the Tower of London.

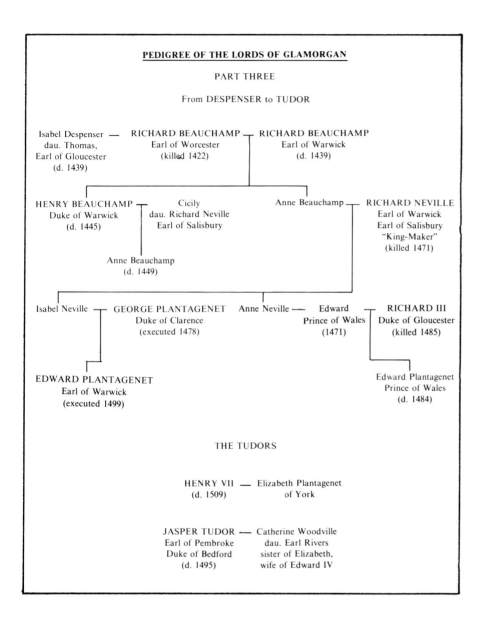

PEDIGREE OF THE LORDS OF GLAMORGAN

PART THREE

From DESPENSER to TUDOR

Isabel Despenser —— RICHARD BEAUCHAMP ─┬─ RICHARD BEAUCHAMP
dau. Thomas, Earl of Worcester   Earl of Warwick
Earl of Gloucester   (killed 1422)   (d. 1439)
(d. 1439)

HENRY BEAUCHAMP ─┬─ Cicily   Anne Beauchamp ─┬─ RICHARD NEVILLE
Duke of Warwick   dau. Richard Neville   Earl of Warwick
(d. 1445)   Earl of Salisbury   Earl of Salisbury
"King-Maker"
(killed 1471)

Anne Beauchamp
(d. 1449)

Isabel Neville ─┬─ GEORGE PLANTAGENET   Anne Neville —— Edward ─┬─ RICHARD III
Duke of Clarence   Prince of Wales   Duke of Gloucester
(executed 1478)   (1471)   (killed 1485)

EDWARD PLANTAGENET   Edward Plantagenet
Earl of Warwick   Prince of Wales
(executed 1499)   (d. 1484)

THE TUDORS

HENRY VII —— Elizabeth Plantagenet
(d. 1509)   of York

JASPER TUDOR —— Catherine Woodville
Earl of Pembroke   dau. Earl Rivers
Duke of Bedford   sister of Elizabeth,
(d. 1495)   wife of Edward IV

Then after fourteen years of imprisonment he had him beheaded on a trumped-up charge of high treason.

Warwick's death was the only judicial murder of Henry's
reign, but his successors were to prove just as ruthless as the
Plantagenets had been.

Three years later, the fourteen year old Princes Arthur was
married to Catherine of Aragon, then a girl of fifteen, but
within a year, in 1502, he was dead. Despite his father's plans, it
was to be yet another Henry who was destined to rule in
Arthur's Britain.

Henry VIII succeeded his father in 1509. Up to that time there had neen no fundamental change in the administration of South Wales. Glamorgan was still a lordship in the sense that the king had a dual capacity, which required him, when dealing with documents concerning the Castle and the Shire, itself, to describe himself as both King of England and Lord of Glamorgan, and to authenticate them under the seal of his Chancery of Cardiff.

This was the procedure until the privileges of the Marcher Lords were abolished by Statute. In 1536 the Union of Wales with England became a legal reality by Act of Parliament and in 1542 Glamorgan became one of the twelve Counties with a Sheriff appointed by the king and represented by two members.

The Herbert Earls of Pembroke

At the court of Henry VII, there had been a Gentleman Usher, Sir Richard Herbert, who became Constable of Abergavenny Castle when Henry VIII succeeded his father. He married Margaret, daughter of Sir Mathew Craddock of Swansea and they had three sons. The eldest, born in 1506, was William.

How William Herbert spent his early days is not known, except that as a young man he visted Bristol and in a brawl on the ancient bridge there, he killed a man.

He wasted no time, but escaped first to South Wales and then to France, where he became a soldier and a great favourite at Court. Subsequently, he returned carrying letters from Francis I recommending him to Henry VIII.

Shortly after the King divorced his first wife, Catherine of Aragon, on the grounds that it was unlawful for him to be married to his late brother's wife, William Herbert wed Anne, daughter of Sir Thomas Parr. This proved to be a very fortunate happening for him, for, in due course, the King married Anne's sister as his sixth and last wife. With the Queen as sister-in-law, it is not surprising that William Herbert prospered.

In 1542, he was granted a coat-of-arms and a crest. He adopted as his motto, "Une je severais" meaning, "One will I serve." In point of fact, he served many, but never more than one at a time, and each of those was to be a Tudor monarch. It says much for his tact and ability that despite the hazards of those times, he not only managed to keep his head when all about him were losing theirs, but he enjoyed the goodwill of each in turn.

He was granted the lands of Wilton Abbey at the Dissolution of the Monastries and there he built a great and beautiful

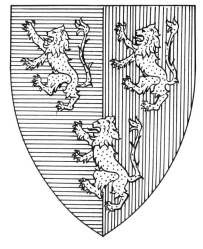

Three golden lions on blue and red. The Herbert Arms.
'Une je severais'.
(One will I serve).

99

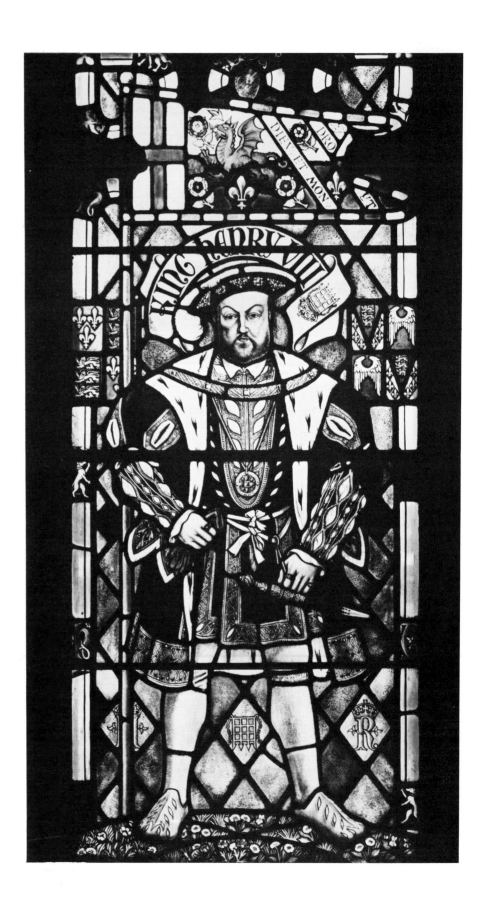

Henry VIII.

residence. At about the same time, his uncle Sir George Herbert of Cogan and Swansea acquired church lands close to Cardiff Castle. On the site of the Greyfriars Convent spared by Owen Glendower he built the grandest house in Glamorgan.

By 1546, William Herbert had become the King's Chief Gentleman of the Privy Chamber, Seneschal of Marlborough, Sulkely, Barton, Devizes, Chilton, and Chippenham, Keeper of Barton's Castle in London and of the Park at Devizes.

He received grants, too, from his sister-in-law, by which he became Receiver General of the Royal Manors of Usk, Caerleon and Trellech. These lands he held with reversion to the King.

He was an executor of the will of Henry VIII and one of the guardians of Edward VI, the ten year old son, who succeeded Henry.

In 1549, there was an insurrection in Devon and Cornwall where discontent with the government of the King's uncle, Edward Seymour, Duke of Somerset, threatened to spread to other parts of the realm. William Herbert was sent to restore order, and so successful was he in doing so, that the young King appointed him President of the Royal Council of Wales and installed him a Knight of the Garter.

In 1551, he received other rewards for his zeal. He became lord of Cardiff Castle, with the titles od Lord Herbert of Cardiff and Earl of Pembroke.

Although it would be incorrect to style him, lord of Glamorgan, his powers and privileges were much the same as those of his predecessors at Cardiff Castle, for the grant of 1551 specifically provided that the lordship should be held by him in as ample a fashion as Jasper Tudor and the other lords of Glamorgan had done as lords of the march.

A few years before William Herbert became lord of Cardiff, the famous travelling historian Leland had passed through and has left us his impression of the town. Freely translated his description shows that Cardiff was surrounded by a wall about a mile in circumference, in which there were five gates. The Ship Gate was to the south leading to the sea and the Water Gate to the south-west by the river. To the north and the north-west, gates led, respectively, to the former lordships of Senghennydd and Miskin. The fifth gate, to the east, was near where North

Road now joins the Kingsway and in those days gave access to Cardiff's biggest suburb, Crockerton.

To the north-west of the town was the castle, itself, partially in ruins. The castle was walled and had two gates, just as it has now. The bigger one was called the Shire Hall Gate and the other, the Exchequer Gate.

There were two great towers, the Keep, or White Tower, used as the King's armoury, and Gilbert de Clare's Black Tower, with its grim dungeon, then in use as a prison. There was also the Shire Hall, itself, the centre of local government.

To the north of the castle, there was a dyke and to the west the River Taff. East of the great ward wall were the ruined buildings, formerly used by Fitzhamon's knights, when on ward duty.

Within the town there had been many religious establishments, but in 1551, after the dissolution of the monastries, there remained only two churches of importance. One was St. Mary's, the former parish church, even then, fast losing the influence it had in former times, and now completely demolished. It was situated approximately where the main railway station now stands. The other was the present parish church of St. John the Baptist, then described as being by the Miskin Gate.

By 1552, both the King's uncles, Thomas, Lord Seymour and the once all powerful Protector, Edward, Duke of Somerset had lost royal favour and been executed. Edward was replaced by John Dudley, Duke of Northumberland, who despite the fact that his own father had been executed early in the reign of Henry VIII, had, like William Herbert, Earl of Pembroke, been appointed one of that king's executors.

Another powerful figure in the kingdom at that time was Henry Grey, Duke of Suffolk. He had married Frances, daughter of Henry VII. They had two daughters, Jane and Katherine.

Jane was married to Lord Guildford Dudley, Northumberland's son and Katherine, to Henry Herbert, son of the Earl of Pembroke. Thus both these young ladies of royal blood were the daughters-in-law of executors of their uncle, Henry VIII.

Northumberland, ever ambitious, persuaded the young Protestant king, Edward VI, to appoint his Protestant cousin, Lady Jane Grey, as his successor to the throne, instead of Mary

Opposite:
The South Gate. The North Gate can be seen in the distance.

103

Tudor, his Catholic half-sister. With Jane queen and his son, Consort, Northumberland's position of power would have been assured.

When Edward died, still only sixteen, in 1553, Suffolk, encouraged by Northumberland, proclaimed his daughter, Lady Jane Grey, Queen of England.

Mary Tudor, however, was not to be brushed aside. She arrived in London with a superior force, was acclaimed by the people, and arrested Jane, whose reign had lasted only a few days.

Four of the first of the many who were to die by execution in the regin of "Bloody Mary" were Lady Jane, herself, her husband, her father and her father-in-law.

Henry Herbert, however, kept his head. He promptly divorced his wife, Lady Katherine Grey. Like his father, he had learned how to live with the Tudors. Subsequently, but not until nearly ten years later, he married again. His second wife was Catherine Talbot, daughter of the Earl of Shrewsbury.

Sir William Herbert continued to enjoy the royal favour, notwithstanding the rapid changes in religious climate. He was at Southampton to greet Philip of Spain, and was present when Queen Mary married him at Winchester in 1554.

In 1557, as Captain General of the English Army to defend Calais, he played a prominent part in the victory gained by Philip over the French at St. Quentin. He outlived Queen Mary and when she died in 1557, served her sister and successor, the great Queen Elizabeth in many high offices, dying at last, greatly honoured and respected at her splendid house, Hampton Court, in 1570.

Henry Herbert succeeded his father as lord of Cardiff Castle and Earl of Pembroke. He prospered in Elizabeth's glorious reign, but his divorced wife, Katherine Grey, did not.

She re-married without the Queen's permission and paid the penalty. She, and her second husband, were both committed to the Tower of London and there, in 1567, she died, leaving three sons.

The husband, who shared part of her imprisonment, was Edward Seymour, Earl of Hertford, son of the Duke of Somerset, the Protector, hanged on Tower Hill by order of his nephew, Edward VI. He was also related to Thomas Seymour of Sudeley, who married Henry VIII's widow Catherine Parr, the sister-in-law of William Herbert, and was, later, a suitor for the hand of the Queen, herself, when she was Princess Elizabeth in the court of her brother.

William Herbert, First Earl of Pembroke.

Henry Herbert, like his father, was a Knight of the Garter and President of the Council of Wales. He was also Lord Lieutenant of South Wales, as well as of Hereford, Shropshire, Somerset, Wiltshire and Worcester. He was a general in the army and an admiral in the navy.

His second wife died in 1575 and two years later he married again. His third wife was Mary, the daughter of Sir Henry Sydney and sister of the poet and courtier who is remembered for the manner of his dying. Mortally wounded at the Battle of Zutphen, as he lay dying, he was handed a cup of water. Untasted, he offered it to another wounded soldier, saying, "Drink, your need is greater than mine."

Encouraged by his wife, Henry Herbert became a great patron of the Arts. They entertained Queen Elizabeth at their home in Wilton, where it is believed Shakespeare and his players first performed at least one of his plays. At Wilton, too, Sir Philip Sydney wrote his "Arcadia" and, in recent times, Sir Winston Churchill painted there.

In 1580, the Countess of Pembroke gave birth to a son, William. The christening was a grand affair. Queen Elizabeth was the godmother and the Earls of Warwick and of Leicester were godfathers. A second son, Philip, was born four years, later.

When William was twenty-one, his father died, and he succeeded to the Earldom of Pembroke and became owner of Cardiff Castle.

That both William and his brother Philip Herbert were, like their father, patrons of the Arts and Letters, is evident, for when the first portfolio of Shakespeare's plays was published in 1623, they were dedicated, "To the most noble and incomparable brothers, William, Earl of Pembroke, Lord Chamberlain to the King's most excellent Majesty, and Philip, Earl of Montgomery, Gentleman of His Majesty's Bedchamber, Both Knights of the Most noble Order of the Garter and our singular good Lords."

This dedication, too, indicates that the Herberts continued to hold high office in the royal household, despite the change of dynasty occasioned by the passing of Elizabeth Tudor and the accession of James Stuart.

In the reign of Charles I, William was appointed Lord

106

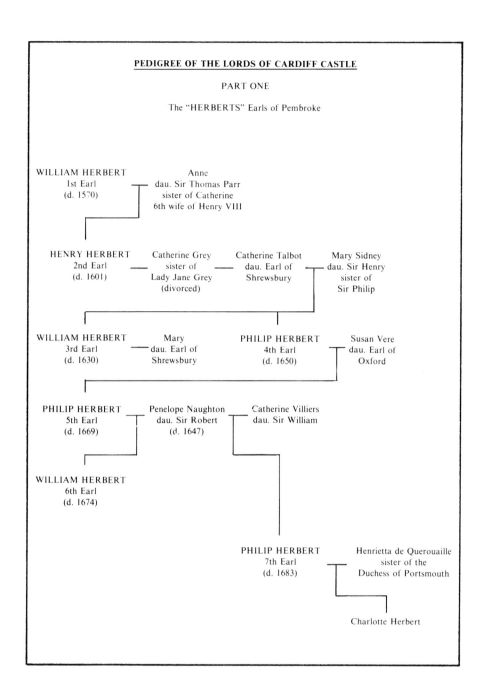

PEDIGREE OF THE LORDS OF CARDIFF CASTLE

PART ONE

The "HERBERTS" Earls of Pembroke

WILLIAM HERBERT
1st Earl
(d. 1570)

Anne
dau. Sir Thomas Parr
sister of Catherine
6th wife of Henry VIII

HENRY HERBERT
2nd Earl
(d. 1601)

Catherine Grey
sister of
Lady Jane Grey
(divorced)

Catherine Talbot
dau. Earl of
Shrewsbury

Mary Sidney
dau. Sir Henry
sister of
Sir Philip

WILLIAM HERBERT
3rd Earl
(d. 1630)

Mary
dau. Earl of
Shrewsbury

PHILIP HERBERT
4th Earl
(d. 1650)

Susan Vere
dau. Earl of
Oxford

PHILIP HERBERT
5th Earl
(d. 1669)

Penelope Naughton
dau. Sir Robert
(d. 1647)

Catherine Villiers
dau. Sir William

WILLIAM HERBERT
6th Earl
(d. 1674)

PHILIP HERBERT
7th Earl
(d. 1683)

Henrietta de Querouaille
sister of the
Duchess of Portsmouth

Charlotte Herbert

Steward, the office the ancestors of the Stuarts, themselves, had held in the courts of earlier dynasties, and from which their name was derived. Philip became Lord Chamberlain.

William had two sons, both by his second wife, but they predeceased him. He died in 1630, and having no direct heir, his brother became Earl of Pembroke, as well as Earl of Mongomery.

He married Susan de Vere, daughter of the Earl of Oxford, and appropriately, succeeded his brother as Chancellor of Oxford University. By her he had a family of nine children. She died in 1628 and he remarried. His second wife was Anne Clifford, heiress of the Earl of Cumberland.

Both William and Philip made many alterations at Wilton, but it is not certain, though probable, that similar work was done, in their time, at Cardiff Castle.

Since Philip was so close to the royal household and had prospered as a result of the favour of the Stuarts, it is surprising that he should have been the first of the Herberts of Cardiff Castle to have failed to live up to the family motto of "One will I serve."

He is unique in another respect, too. All the other lords of Cardiff Castle, from the days of Robert Consul, had fought for, or against, the king in times of civil war. He appears to have taken no active part in the struggle between Charles and Parliament, although his sympathies are thought to have been with the aspirations of Cromwell.

He had spent his life in peaceful pursuits and had neither the training nor the temperament for war. Furthermore, the enforcement of the Statutes of Livery and Maintenance had deprived the great lords of their former right to maintain private armies recognisable by the livery they wore.

Consequently, even had he wished to, Philip could not have mustered a force to compare in size and power with those of Warwick the Kingmaker, or of his own ancestor, Sir William Herbert of Raglan Castle during the Wars of the Roses in which both had died.

Philip Herbert was out of step, too, with the general trend in the kingdom, for the King found most of his supporters from the ranks of the landowners in the west and the north. In Glamorgan, Philip was not alone in favouring the Parliamentarians during what came to be known as the "Great Rebellion," but he was certainly in a minority so far as his own class was concerned.

Prominent among those who remained faithful to the royal cause were Philip's relatives, the descendants of Sir George Herbert, who had obtained the site of the Greyfriars on which had been built their magnificent house. One of them, William

Herbert, member of Parliament representing the Cardiff Boroughs, fought and died for the King at the Battle of Edgehill in 1642.

It was from the family of the Greyfriars Herberts that the Constable of Cardiff Castle was almost invariably appointed. This was an important post for he acted as mayor of the town as the deputy of the Earl of Pembroke, and as such exercised considerable influence on local affairs. Although in theory it was the bailiffs and aldermen who governed the town no one was elected to these offices without his approval.

There are many stories told of the struggle for the control of Cardiff Castle during the Great Rebellion. Some of them have been embellished in the course of the years and others are largely fictional.

According to one of them, Cromwell, himself, took the stronghold in 1642, after bombarding it from across the river. It is said that entry was forced by a small party of roundheads, who used a secret subterranean passage under the Taff, and that the traitor, who disclosed the underground way, was executed by Cromwell, when he demanded his thirty pieces of silver.

There is no evidence, however, that such a passage ever existed. Nor that Cromwell was ever in Cardiff. He seems much more likely that the Earl of Pembroke was unable, or unwilling, to oppose the occupation of the Castle by the Parliamentary forces.

What is certain, is that shortly after this exploit is supposed to have happened, the Marquess of Hertford, with a party of Cavaliers, crossed the Bristol Channel from Minehead and in a surprise attack retook the Castle for the King. In this, he may have been assisted by the Constable, an elderly member of the Greyfriars Herberts.

This Marquess of Hertford was the grandson of Sir Edward Seymour, the nephew of Jane Seymour, mother of Edward VI, who had incurred the wrath of Queen Elizabeth by marrying without her consent the unfortunate Katherine Grey, sister of Lady Jane, and the divorced wife of Philip Herberts father, Henry.

It seems likely that Cardiff Castle was captured again by the Cromwellians. One of their despatches states that this was effected with the help of the men of Glamorgan in an engagement of five hours at a cost of nine men killed against the fifty lost by the Royalists. These figures seem doubtful, since the king's men were behind strong defences, unless once again the Parliamentarians were aided by treachery from within the garrison.

The course of events from that time on are even more difficult to ascertain. One authority states that the Cromwellians continued to hold the Castle from 1642 to 1645 when the High Sheriff of Glamorgan changed his allegiance and captured Cardiff for the King. He was not able to take the Castle, though, according to another Parliamentarian dispatch because, "there were godly and faithful officers there."

Nevertheless, it was in royalist hands in the summer of 1645, because Charles I is known to have dined in the Castle soon after his defeat at Naseby. This tends to confirm another source that it was held for the King for the greater part of the period of the Great Rebellion.

The most serious fighting took place in 1648 after the Castle had been retaken by Cromwell's men. The battle was fought to the west of Cardiff near the site of the old Norman castle of Sir Peter le Sor, one of the twelve knight-companions of Robert Fitzhamon.

On the 8th May the royalist forces under the command of General Laugharne opposed a smaller but better trained army led by Colonel Horton, who had arrived on the scene after a gruelling forced march of forty miles over hilly country from Brecon.

The Cavaliers were completely routed and annihilated. The slaughter was such, that the Rhyd Laver, the stream at the bottom of the slope, flowed red with blood. Three thousand prisoners were taken and large quantities of arms and ammunition were captured. It was, by far, the most important engagement in Glamorgan, if not in Wales, during the whole period of the civil war.

Charles I was beheaded on the 30th January 1649 and within a year the Earl of Pembroke died, too, and was succeeded by his son, Philip.

The fifth Earl of Pembroke, Philip Herbert, was the second son of his father. His elder brother, christened Charles, in honour of the king, had died of smallpox in Italy in 1635.

Philip Herbert is thought to have been on the side of the King during the period of the Great Rebellion, but in spite of this, perhaps in recognition of his father's sympathies for the rebels, no action was taken either against the Earl or his properties when Cromwell became Lord Protector. Cardiff Castle had suffered severe damage during the hostilities but no attempt to destroy it was made afterwards. Others were less fortunate. Action was taken against both Bristol and Caerphilly Castles. Of the former, nothing now remains.

The Earl lived on throughout the period of the commonwealth and at the Restoration of the Monarchy, he, like his forebears, became prominent at court, being privileged to bear the spurs of the Merry Monarch at his coronation.

He married twice, to Penelope, daughter of Sir Robert Naughton and to Catherine, daughter of Sir William Villiers. By Penelope he had one son, William and by Catherine seven children including two sons, Philip and Thomas. He died in 1669 and was succeeded by William.

The sixth Earl of Pembroke and third Earl of Montgomery was of a quiet, retiring nature. He had been born in 1640 and spent his youth in the disturbing atmosphere of civil war. At the age of seven there had been a devastating fire at Wilton, where the home of his grandfather and its priceless contents had been almost completely destroyed. Two years later came the shocking news that the King had been executed. These events, undoubtedly, effected him profoundly. He never married and died on the 8th July 1674, being succeeded by his half-brother, Philip.

The seventh Earl was a dissolute spend-thrift with a streak of violence in his nature. Cardiff was fortunate in that the new lord of the Castle was seldom, if ever, there. He lived mainly in London and it was there that he was involved in brawls that resulted in the death of at least two men.

Twice charged with murder, he was tried, as was his right, by his fellow peers, who acquitted him of the major charge but found him guilty of manslaughter. He was committed to the Tower of London, eventually being pardoned and released by order of Charles II, whose mistress, Louise, Duchess of Portsmouth, was the sister of Henriette de Querouaille, Philip Herbert's wife.

In 1678, two men of very different character, were imprisoned in the Black Tower at Cardiff Castle. It was the year of the so called Popist Plot, when Titus Oates, professing to be a Roman Catholic, but really out to discredit them, spread the tale of the existence of a plot which he said was to murder Charles II in order to replace him setting his Roman Catholic brother, James, on the throne in his stead.

Feelings ran high and a new act, a development from the earlier Test Acts, which prohibited the holding of high office by Roman Catholics or Puritans, was passed. It provided for the punishment of persons who persisted in exercising offices prohibited to those who refused to take the "Test" and declare their willingness to receive, or in the case of a priest to administer, the sacraments in accordance with the rites of the Church of England.

Father Philip Evans was arrested under the new Act and kept in solitary confinement in the dungeon of the Black Tower for three weeks. Father John Lloyd was also arrested and similarly charged. As an act of grace they were allowed to spend their last few days together, presumably in the larger room on the ground floor of the Tower. Even there, it is stated, the air became so foul that they were obliged to stand close to the grating in order to breath. In the end they were executed in the most revolting manner. Their bowels were taken out and burned, their heads were cut off and their bodies were quartered.

Philip Herbert, the seventh Earl died on the 29th August 1683, leaving to his only child, Charlotte, his Welsh estates including Cardiff Castle. The Earldoms of Pembroke and Montgomery passed to his brother, Thomas.

During the ownership of Cardiff Castle by the Herbert family, the lodgings along the west wall had been considerably extended and modified. The Great Hall of Richard Beauchamp had been divided into two rooms by partitioning and a new northern wing had been addded. The two rooms were then called the Hall and the Middle Room. In the wing was the Upper Room and the Butler's apartment with a kitchen and pantries.

On the south side of the Great Hall, a small Entrance Hall, ten feet wide, was built. It protruded beyond the general line of the old frontage. When this was completed, the old entrance, giving direct access into the south end of the Great Hall, was blocked up.

Immediately behind the new Entrance Hall, and accessible to it by way of the Great Hall and a new passage-way out through the thickness of the old Norman wall, was built another tower, the Herbert Tower. It was similar in size, both as to height and width to the Beauchamp Octagonal Tower but of square construction and containing more and bigger windows. There was a space of approximately twenty feet between the two towers and, consequently, the Herbert Tower extended along the outside of the wall to the south beyond the extremity of the Entrance Hall extension on the inner side.

Lady Charlotte Herbert married John, Lord Jeffreys, in July 1668. He was of ancient Welsh lineage and the son of one of the most powerful men in the kingdom, Baron Jeffreys of Wem. He was a Privy Councillor, Lord Chief Justice of the King's Bench, Lord High Chancellor of England and Lord Steward of England. In history, however, he is better known as Judge Jeffreys

The Entrance Hall.

of the Bloody Assizes; the ruthless judge who had brought terror, torture and death to hundreds of West Countrymen, and others, accused of having taken part in Monmouth's abortive rebellion against James II.

Following the wedding, events moved fast for it was the year of the Glorious Revolution. In the November William, Prince of Orange, landed at Brixham and advanced on London. James II abdicated, was deposed and went into exile all within a period of two months.

Judge Jeffreys tried to leave, too, but he was recognised boarding a collier at Newcastle, was brought back to London, imprisoned in the Tower and there he died.

Compared with his father, Lord Jeffreys had an uneventful life. He had one daughter, by Lady Charlotte, who married, Thomas, Earl of Pomfret but had no rights in connection with Cardiff Castle. Lord Jeffreys died in 1702 and a year later his widow married again.

Charlotte Herbert's second husband was the younger brother of the Earl of Plymouth. He was Thomas, Viscount Windsor, a soldier who had served with the first Churchill, the Duke of Marlborough, in Flanders. In recognition of his distinguished career he was honoured by Queen Anne, who created him Baron Mountjoy in the Isle of Wight. He had one son, christened appropriately, Herbert Windsor, and three daughters.

Charlotte Herbert died in 1733, and was succeeded by the son, Herbert Windsor as Lord of Cardiff Castle. When his father died, five years later, Herbert Windsor became Viscount Windsor and Baron Mountjoy.

He married Alice, daughter of Sir John Clavering and co-heir of Sir James Clavering, Baronet. They had two daughters, Charlotte-Jane, born on 7th May 1746 and Alice-Elizabeth, who were co-heirs of their father's estates when he died in 1758.

Meanwhile, there were repercussions in Cardiff caused by the Seven Years War, which was to gain Britain an Empire. The Prime Minister of the day, John, third Earl of Bute, wished to utilise Cardiff Castle as a prison for captured French soldiers. This proposal was welcomed neither by Lady Windsor nor the people of Cardiff.

In 1766, the Earl of Bute's son, John, Lord Mount Stuart married Lady Windsor's daughter, Charlotte-Jane. Her younger sister married too, but both she and her infant daughter died, after which event Alice's share in the estates was purchased by the trustees of Charlotte-Jane.

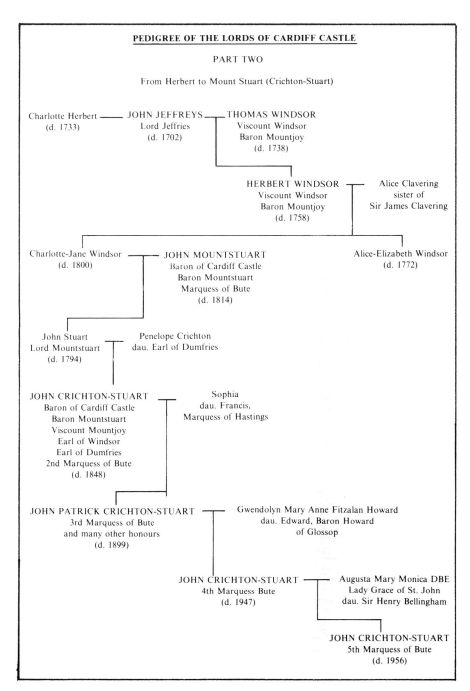

PEDIGREE OF THE LORDS OF CARDIFF CASTLE

PART TWO

From Herbert to Mount Stuart (Crichton-Stuart)

Charlotte Herbert —— JOHN JEFFREYS —— THOMAS WINDSOR
(d. 1733)   Lord Jeffries   Viscount Windsor
                   (d. 1702)   Baron Mountjoy
                                  (d. 1738)

HERBERT WINDSOR —— Alice Clavering
Viscount Windsor   sister of
Baron Mountjoy   Sir James Clavering
(d. 1758)

Charlotte-Jane Windsor —— JOHN MOUNTSTUART   Alice-Elizabeth Windsor
(d. 1800)   Baron of Cardiff Castle   (d. 1772)
                     Baron Mountstuart
                     Marquess of Bute
                         (d. 1814)

John Stuart   Penelope Crichton
Lord Mountstuart   dau. Earl of Dumfries
(d. 1794)

JOHN CRICHTON-STUART   Sophia
Baron of Cardiff Castle   dau. Francis,
Baron Mountstuart   Marquess of Hastings
Viscount Mountjoy
Earl of Windsor
Earl of Dumfries
2nd Marquess of Bute
(d. 1848)

JOHN PATRICK CRICHTON-STUART —— Gwendolyn Mary Anne Fitzalan Howard
3rd Marquess of Bute   dau. Edward, Baron Howard
and many other honours   of Glossop
(d. 1899)

JOHN CRICHTON-STUART —— Augusta Mary Monica DBE
4th Marquess Bute   Lady Grace of St. John
(d. 1947)   dau. Sir Henry Bellingham

JOHN CRICHTON-STUART
5th Marquess of Bute
(d. 1956)

Introduction to the Bute Period

After the death of the 7th Earl of Pembroke, the long association of the surname, Herbert, with Cardiff Castle ceased, but the blood kinship continued through the female line.

With the marriage of the 7th Earl's great-granddaughter to Lord Mount-Stuart, another, and the last, family name was added to the list of the resident lords of Cardiff Castle. Better known locally as the Marquess of Bute, the Stuart family had come a long way from their ancestral home in Scotland.

In 1627, Sir James Stuart, a kinsman, and a zealous supporter of Charles I, had been created a baronet. His grandson was raised to the peerage of Scotland, as Earl of Bute, by Queen Anne, 1703, after holding the office of Privy Councillor and acting as Commisioner appointed to negotiate the Union of Scotland with the rest of Great Britain.

The 1st Earl's grandson, a friend of George III, was Prime Minister and First Lord of the Treasury in 1762/3. His son, it was, who married Charlotte Jane Windsor, the heiress of Cardiff Castle.

At that time, the Industrial Revolution had scarcely begun in England. Wales was then an agricultural and pastoral country where all the valleys were green. Cardiff, itself, was a town with no more than three hundred residential buildings housing approximately one thousand people.

Politically, prospects were bright. The Hanoverian dynasty had grown to maturity after having successfully survived the teething troubles of the reigns of the first two monarchs, George I and George II. The Jacobite Rebellions and the Seven Years War were both part of history. Britain had emerged stronger than ever before and found herself Mother Country of a great empire that included vast areas of Canada and India as well as the American Colonies.

From the arrival of the Butes, until they relinquished their ownership of the Castle in 1948, was a time of unpresidented expansion in Cardiff, unequalled, possibly anywhere else on earth.

With a population of 1870 in 1801, it increased to 6187 by 1831, to 221,500 by 1936 and to 259,700 by 1966.

By comparison, Carmarthen, the largest town in Wales in 1801, had only about 12,000 people one hundred and fifty years later. Merthyr Tydfil, the most populous town in Glamorgan,

First Marquess of Bute.

117

in 1801, grew from 7,705 people in 1801, to 22,000 in 1831 and to approximately 60,000 in the year 1961.

Of the total population of Wales, about one half live in Glamorgan and half of those in the three towns of Cardiff, Swansea and Merthyr. Cardiff, alone, is greater in population than both Swansea and Merthyr combined. That is the measure of the growth of the town since 1801. This was not attributable to natural increase, alone, but was the result of employment opportunities and living conditions in Cardiff becoming so much more attractive than elsewhere.

Immigrants flooded in from other parts of Wales, from England and, above all, from Ireland. They came from more distant parts, as well. They included West Indian and Arab seamen, who married local women and settled in Tiger Bay. It was this influx then that accounts for the cosmopolitan character of the Cardiffian of today.

These immigrants provided the labour for the building of the roads, canals and railways. They built the docks too, which had to be excavated on reclaimed mud flats, for Cardiff had no natural sea port facilities. These great works were necessary to transport the high quality coal which the Welsh produced for half the world.

At about the time the Butes arrived in Cardiff, the town was described by Lord Camden as "A proper fine town (as towns in this country go) and a very commodious haven", and by that time, the castle had ceased to be the centre of actual warfare. Those days were long passed. It was no longer the shield of the Roman soldier with a short broad sword prepared to conquer or to die. It had become, instead, more a grand town house of a time-expired general living in honourable retirement.

The time, alas, was not an era of everlasting peace — far from it. Bigger conflicts were still fought but the scene had shifted to more distant foreign fields.

Within a long-bow shot of the castle walls in Cardiff are memorials, a house and two statues, to three men who served in very different ways in the Great War of 1914/18 when the Welsh and the English fought, not as adversaries, but side by side as brothers in arms in defence of the British Empire.

In the house was born a later-day bard, Ivor Novello, whose

118

songs were sung by millions of marching men leaving behind their women and children to "Keep the Home Fires Burning."

The statues are memorials to two men of very different origins. One from a humble home, David Lloyd George, who rose to be Prime Minister and triumphant war-time leader. The other might well have become Lord of the Castle if he had survived. Like his ancestors, he went to war and died on active service.

Second Marquess of Bute.

CHAPTER TWELVE

The Marquesses of Bute

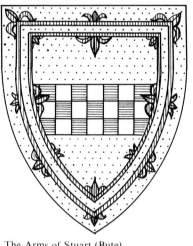

The Arms of Stuart (Bute).
'Avita virs honore'.
(He flourishes through the honour of his ancestors).

Lord Mount Stuart was created Baron Cardiff of Cardiff Castle in 1776. In the same year, he decided that the great ward wall built in the days of the Clares, connecting the Keep to the Black Tower, should be removed. This proved to be a most formidable task and was finally accomplished only after gunpowder had been used. The old medieval buildings in the outer ward were demolished, too, as well as the old Shire Hall.

Naturally, there were antiquarians who regretted the destruction of such ancient monuments as the ruins of the lodgings of Fitzhamon's knights, but, if, as was his intention, the Castle was to be used again as a residence, their removal was essential in order to admit light and air into the rooms.

In 1777, both Robert Adams and Lancelot — better known as "Capability" — Brown, two of the most eminent architects of the day, were invited to submit proposals and estimates for the complete transformation of the hybrid conglomeration of buildings of different periods along the west wall of the Castle.

Robert Adams had very ambitious plans for an elaborate and expensive building. Brown's were simpler and his estimate lower. He it was who was commissioned to put in hand the necessary work.

Practically everything added to the Great Hall since the time of Jasper Tudor, with the exception of the Herbert Tower, was demolished. Two new matching wings were constructed increasing the frontage of the building to approximately 170 feet. In the northern wing there was a new drawing room and in the southern one, a new kitchen and pantry. The interior changes cannot now be identified because they have suffered alteration during subsequent rebuilding activities. From engravings that

Cardiff Castle, Rowlandson Aquatint, 1799.
(National Museum of Wales).

still exist, however, it is evident that Capability Brown was very successful in marrying the new with the old thereby producing a pleasing, harmonious and elegant residence, enhanced by the trees planted and the lawns laid in the courtyard.

The Castle was little used by the family in the time of Lord Mount Stuart because the approach to it was cluttered up with small houses. Although he had entered into negotiations to buy them, intending afterwards to remove them, he was not able to bring his plans to a satisfactory conclusion.

His father died in 1792 and he then succeeded him as fourth Earl of Bute; his own son, John Stuart, then only twenty-five years old, the Member of Parliament for Cardiff and the Contributary Boroughs of Glamorgan becoming Lord Mount Stuart.

This son, who had recently married, had a son born on 10th August 1793 and was killed falling from his horse on the 22nd January 1794.

This sad event was a great sorrow for the Earl of Bute, and

Cardiff Castle, Metcalf Etching, *c*.1785.
(National Museum of Wales).

since he had intended the restored Castle to be the residence of his son, further work on it was abandoned.

In 1794, Lord Bute's mother died. He then succeeded her in the Barony of Mount Stuart and two years later was created Viscount of Mountjoy in the Isle of Wight, Earl of Windsor and Marquess of Bute. His first wife, Charlotte-Jane, died on the 28th January 1800, after which event he married Frances Coutts, daughter of the banker. She brought him to title but a princely dowry which was to be used by the Butes in the development of Cardiff.

The first Marquess of Bute died in 1814, the year before Wellington won the Battle of Waterloo and ended at last the invasion scare that had been a very real one in South Wales ever since the French had succeeded in landing an armed force in Pembrokeshire in 1797.

122

John Crichton-Stuart, whose father had died when he was only a few months old, succeeded his paternal grandfather as second Marquess of Bute, Viscount of Mountjoy and Earl of Windsor, just as he had succeeded to the Earldom of Dumfries and assumed the additional surname of Crichton when his maternal grandfather died in 1803. There was one title, however, that he did not inherit, he earned. He became known as the "Father of modern Cardiff." This was because he, its first citizen, was largely responsible for developing the coalfields and building the docks which resulted in Cardiff, a town with a population of little more than 1,000 when he was born, becoming the greatest coal port in the world.

He married Sophia, the daughter of Francis, Marquess of Hastings and after making the Castle habitable again abandoned Cathay's House, the Cardiff residence built by his grandfather, and lived there.

When he inherited it, both the buildings and the grounds were in a somewhat delapidated condition. Nearly forty years had passed since the "Capability" Brown restorations and meanwhile it had been used for housing prisoners of war as well as a training ground for British soldiers. Sheep had grazed within its walls and townsfolk had been allowed to use the rampart walls from which they could enjoy the view of the pre-industrial age countryside. The grandiose scheme to convert and utilise the Keep as a grand ball-room with a gigantic copper roof, chandeliers and pier-glass had long since been abandoned and left ivy-covered and infested with weeds so that even the pathway spiralling upwards around the mound was difficult to find.

Among the additions built by the second Marquess was a dressing-room built on to the Octagonal Tower in the space between it and the Herbert Tower which was by then being used as a study. It was in this dressing room that he died suddenly and alone at the age of fifty five on the 18th March 1848, less than one year after the birth of his son.

It was a tragic co-incidence that both the second and the third Marquess of Bute should have been bereaved in early infancy so that neither of them could remember his own father.

John Patrick Crichton-Stuart, third Marquess of Bute, came of age in 1868 and almost at once declared his conversion from

The Octagonal Tower's lead covered
wooden spire, the work of William
Burgess.

the Presbyterian faith of his parents to Roman Catholicism. Since the days of the "Test Acts" had long since passed, the event caused nothing more than a mild sensation. In 1872, he married Gwendoline Mary, daughter of Edward, Baron Howard of Glossop, and continued the work of his father in the development of Cardiff, becoming mayor of the town in 1880, shortly before the birth of his son and heir.

As Cardiff, itself, is the true memorial of the second Marquess so Cardiff Castle, in its present form, is the monument of his son.

During his lifetime, it was completely transformed and the fact of Roman occupation on the site proved. His architect, William Burgess, famous for other large projects, including at least one Catheral, was responsible for work in Australia, as well as in Ireland and in the United Kingdom. In addition to Cardiff Castle, he was commissioned by the Marquess to re-build the Castell Goch.

Just as the work of previous generations was demolished in the reconstruction work of "Capability" Brown, so his own disappeared in the transformation wrought by Burgess for the third Marquess.

Vast structural alterations were made. Three new towers were built, as well as new stabling, increasing the extent of the buildings along the west wall considerably. The Norman south wall that extended only from the angle with the west wall to the main entrance opposite High Street, was rebuilt, too.

The Bute Tower, built on the extreme north end of the west wall structure, was reached via the drawing-room of the Capability Brown period through yet another way cut through the thickness of the wall. Like the Beauchamp and the Herbert Towers, it protruded from the outer side of the wall.

The new Clock Tower was built on the other extreme, on the corner site where the west and the south walls meet, while the Guest Tower, constructed entirely within the line of the wall and flush with the Great Hall on the inner side of the building, was separated from it by a new Entrance Hall, replacing the earlier one that had led straight into the northern end of the Great Hall.

The central partition that had divided the great Hall into two rooms since the Herbert period was removed and a ceiling-floor constructed to form a large library with a banqueting hall above it.

During the second half of the nineteenth century, rich industrialists built residences incorporating castle features that would never be used in war on sites remote from any scene of conflict.

The third Marquess of Bute reversed that process. He converted his ancient castle into a rich Victorian residence, even to the extent of beautifying it, according to the taste of his age. Thus, when he built the colourful, ornate Clock Tower, he also surmounted the grim, mural, octagonal tower of Richard Beauchamp with the magnificent and delightful spire of lead covered wood complete with a coronet thereby softening the harsh characteristics of a fortress.

The Towers of Cardiff Castle as seen from Bute Park. From left to right are the Bute Tower, the Herbert Tower, the Octagonal Tower of Beauchamp of Warwick, the Guest Tower, the Clock Tower.

The Guest Tower.

The Clock Tower

In Friary Gardens, near the site of the old North Gate of the town, in the former suburb of Crockerton, stands the statue of the third Marquess of Bute. It shows him as a man of great physical presence. The cold grey stone, however, tells nothing of his mind. In this respect, the style of his decoration of the interior of the nearby castle is much more illuminating.

A hint of what can be found inside is given by the seventy feet high Clock Tower. Built in the romanticised style of the Middle Ages, complete with turrets reminicent of the Tower housing Big Ben in the Palace of Westminster it is resplendant with the tinctures of heraldry and the colours of the firmament. Family shields those of Herbert, Crichton, Stuart, Montagu and Windsor view with representations of the sun, moon and stars, the signs of the zodiac and the planets.

In the library, a magnificent room seventy five feet long and twenty three feet wide, there are now no books, but the size of the book-cases and the names of the authors around the walls indicate the number and variety of the volumes that were once there.

It was from these books that the mind of the Marquess drew its inspiration. It was from the family motto, "Avito viret honore", (He flourishes with ancient honour) on the crest in the centre of the fire grate, that gave it direction. The decorations feature the men associated with the castle from the earliest times and honours their memory. None are omitted.

Roman walling is carefully preserved and the culture of the Romans lavishly illustrated. In the library, together with the arms attributed to the early Welsh Princes, including those of the legendary Arthur, are the banners of Roman Emperors and high up in the Summer Smoke Room at the top of the lofty Clock Tower, dominating the room, is Apollo, their sun-god, gilded and glistening in the centre of a chandelier of sun-rays reflected by bevelled-glass mirrors and surrounded by stars. Below him are the lesser Roman gods and heroes associated with the heavens. Their legends, how they came to be placed in the sky forming the constellations, are told in hand-painted illustrations on tiles all round the room.

The Norman relics were retained, too, the Mound, the Keep, the banking and the Black Tower. The west and the south wall were refaced where necessary. Embrasures and arrow slits, as well as a reconstructed hourd of timber from which defenders could have dropped missiles on to assailants below, were added, all of them typical Norman defence features.

Within the Castle, the Normans, together with the other Lords of Glamorgan from Robert Fitzhamon to Henry VIII, with their ladies, were depicted in armour and ceremonial dress

The Library.

including the shields and the armorial bearings attributed to them, in glowing stained-glass set in the bays built in the Great Hall by Jasper Tudor. Presented in chronological order from left to right all the Normans, as well as the Clares and the first of the Despensers, are to be seen in the Banqueting Hall. Representations of the later lords are in what are now other

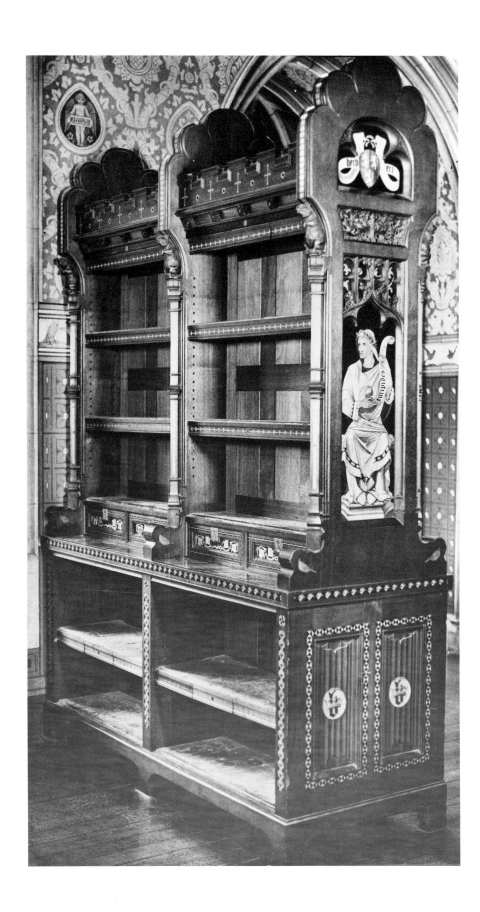

A Library Bookshelf.

rooms extending along the face of the building, the last ones being situated in the Entrance Hall.

Robert Consul, the half-Welsh half-Norman lord is given great prominence for scenes from his life are depicted in stone over the fireplace and in more than twenty mural paintings by the famous fresco artist H. N. Lonsdale.

Monuments to the Medievalists are in the Great Hall, itself, now the library and the Banqueting Hall and, of course, the Octogonal Tower of Richard Beauchamp, Earl of Warwick. This was converted from a grim adjunct of the walled Castle into a receptacle of art and beauty. The old guard room now the Chaucer Room, is in the upper part of the Tower, the Grand Staircase being below it.

Geoffrey Chaucer, the "Father of English Verse", was living in the days of Owen Glendower, whose rebellion and attack on Cardiff Castle was the reason for the Tower having to be built, and is represented in marble. His main works, including his "Canterbury Tales" are illustrated in paint and in stained-glass.

The memorial to the Earls of Pembroke is the Herbert Tower which contains the Arab Room, probably the richest gem in the Castle. With its beautiful marble floor and walls, it is embellished with exotic carving both in wood and stone picked out with gold leaf and lapis lazuli.

The dressing room, where the second Marquess died, suddenly and alone, was converted by his son into a beautiful memorial chapel in his honour. In it, he placed a marble bust of the father he never knew facing the impressive altar representing in gilt and marble the tomb of Christ guarded by soldiers and tended by angels. The vaulted roof and upper walls are covered with paintings from the New Testament and the mosaic floor and the lower walls are of marble. Around them as everywhere else in the Castle are shields of the former lords of Cardiff Castle.

Wood carving of the highest quality is to be found in many apartments, especially in the Library, the Banqueting Hall, the Dining Room and the Chaucer Room. Birds, insects, and creatures of all kinds from crocodiles to monkeys are carved in wood, and in stone. Aesop's fables are told in wall paintings besides the Grand Staircase and high up above the staircase on the Bute Tower. From the ridiculous to the sublime, Old Testament

Detail from a Library Bookshelf.

133

The Summer Smoke Room.

scenes decorate the Dining Room and the Roof Garden. Resplendant with flowers, enamelled tiles and fountains, the windows of the garden overlook the Ladies Walk, the Moat and Bute Park, and far away can be seen the Caerphilly Mountains and, nestling in woodland, the Castell Coch, another of the castles restored by the third Marquess and William Burgess. Sophia Gardens, too, are near-by, once part of the Bute estates but presented to Cardiff in 1858, a year before the death of the Countess Sophia, when her son, the third Marquess was twelve years old.

In 1889, the decorations in the Chaucer Room, the last to be undertaken, were completed by Messrs. Campbell, Smith and Company. The Marquess then turned his attentions to the gardens. In particular he wished to construct a large imposing

Detail from murals in the Banqueting Hall.

The Great Hall.

138

gateway on the northern side of the site. Part of the eastern banking was removed to make a passage from the Castle to the gardens on the opposite side of the North Road. By doing so, he lay bare the lower part of a wall from four feet to five feet high and about ten feet thick of squared, hammer dressed masonry

Opposite:
Apollo. Summer Smoke Room.

The Chapel, formerly the dressing room.

The Arab Room. Fireplace with the
Crichton-Stuart Coat of Arms.

supported by octagonal buttresses or mural turrets. It was evident from the position, and workmanship, as well as by the type of stone used, that it was Roman walling. Probing proved that it extended continously on the northern and eastern sides. It was then assumed, as was later proved, that it continued on the south and on the west as well. It was a most exciting discovery.

The Chaucer Room.

141

In 1894, the area of Roath Park with its beautiful artificial lake was acquired for public use. It had originally been farm land used for supplying the needs of the garrison and had been held by the lords of the Castle since ancient times.

Shortly before his death in 1899, the third Marquess sold the parkland of what had been his grandfather's residence, Cathay's House. On it was built the magnificent Civic Centre complex, which included the City Hall, the Law Courts, the National Museum of Wales as well as University buildings.

When he died at the age of 53, he was succeeded by his elder son, John Crichton-Stuart, who made some relatively small alterations and additions to the Castle, itself, and vast improvements to its appearance from the outside.

At the turn of the century, there was no wall visible from the Main Entrance of the Castle along Duke Street, which was narrow with shops and other buildings on both sides of it, some of which occupied the area now comprising the broad green verge in front of the walls, the pavement and more than half the present width of the road.

Buildings adjoined the Castle Gateway, itself, and extended in the direction of the High Street, opposite which there was a substantial Corner House.

In 1921, in a clearance operation all these buildings were demolished and the road widened. It then became possible for the fourth Marquess of Bute to undertake the building of the present wall.

It was then that a most important discovery was made. The finest example of Roman walling in Britain was uncovered. Approximately, 270 feet long of an average height of twelve feet and up to ten feet thick, it extended from the present Entrance, formerly the Southern Gateway of the Roman Castrum, to the junction of Castle Street and Kingsway.

Nothing of this wonderful find was destroyed. Instead, a wall of Roman type construction, complete with bastions, was built on the remains of the old, and in order that there should never be any confusion as to which part was original work, a course of red stone was set on top of the Roman lias limestone, effectively separating it from the mountain limestone which was then used to complete it.

Opposite:
The Arab Room ceiling.

143

Furthermore, to preserve the Roman workmanship, and to ensure that it could be inspected in comfort, along the inner side of the wall, a roofed corridor was constructed, under the banking, six feet, three inches wide. Access to it could be gained by an entrance close to the Gate Lodge.

The wall, then reconstructed in the Roman style, extends

Third Marquess of Bute.

from the eastern side of the Entrance Gateway to Kingsway, where at a short distance from the angle of the wall it joins similar walling previously reconstructed.

With the completion of this section, once again after a lapse of many centuries, the whole area of the Roman site was enclosed by walls. The Normans had, at no time, walled in more than the western half of the site. Their walling, in part reconstructed by the third Marquess, still exists from the Main Entrance to the Clock Tower and then along the western side of the Castle to the Bute Tower and the section from it, surmounted by the Ladies Walk, ending at the small tower which is the focal point where the Norman and the Roman type walling meet. From this tower, too, a reconstructed wall extends on the inner side following the line of the Norman wall of the Clare period which crodded the moat and thence upwards over the mound to the Shell Keep.

Altogether, the walls of Cardiff Castle are approximatelyhalf a mile in circumference and from the ground level of the Roman period, about thirty five feet high. The western wall bows outwards slightly following the original course of the River Taff. It is about 230 yards long. Both it, and its eastern counterpart, is longer than those on the other two sides. They are each about 194 yards in length. The banking to the north, the east and the south-east of the site are between twenty five and thirty five feet high and from fifty to seventy feet broad at the base. The total area enclosed is about 8 acres and the whole plot was at one time surrounded by broad ditches or moats.

In 1921, under the shadow of the Beauchamp Tower, built to protect it, the old West Gate of the town was reconstructed in the style and on the actual site of the one destroyed by Owen Glendower in 1404.

Two years later, the Northern Gateway of the Castle was reconstructed, too. Care was taken to rebuild it on the foundations and in the form thought to have been used by the Romans, whose cohorts passed out through such an exit, centuries ago, to march along the great highway, the Via Julia.

For the energetic and the romantic, the view from the top of the Keep should not be missed. Nobody nowadays will threaten them with arrow, boulder or boiling oil, as in former times, and

An altar piece recently discovered in the Castle.

crossing the moat, though twenty feet deep presents no problem or danger.

The mound, sixty yards in diameter at the base and thirty three yards across at the table summit thirty five feet up, is a

146

good place to rest and look. From that height the eye can follow the line of the dwarf walls built to indicate the position of the demolished ward wall of Gilbert de Clare which stretched from the Black Tower to the Keep marking the eastern extent of the Norman walled defences. To the left of it are the banks and the reconstructed wall which indicate the eastern limit of the Roman Castrum. To the right of it is the Norman wall, marking the western limit common to both defence systems, along which the buildings of Cardiff Castle have developed since the days of Richard Beauchamp of Warwick.

Between the dwarf and the eastern wall was the outer ward and in it the lodgings of Fitzhamon's knights were situated as well as a church and the Shire Hall.

Safe within the Shell Keep it is evident, as the name implies, that it consists only of massive encircling walls. They tower thirty feet high around the great courtyard seventy seven feet across against which in former times timber buildings stood.

From the Entrance Tower of the Clare period, or from the Watch Tower, spectacular views can be seen of a Cardiff the early builders never dreamed of, including the Civic Centre and the lofty office block erected on the site of the Greyfriars. Sophisticated though they are, who can say that the ancient Keep may not endure long after these modern structures have been demolished and forgotten.

On the 24th June 1948, shortly after the death of the fourth Marquess of Bute, his son gave the Castle to the Corporation, for the benefit of the people of Cardiff.

During its long history it has been stormed many times, and armed men have risked life and liberty to gain admittance. In these happier days when even the Keep, itself, is guarded by nothing more formidable than swans and peacocks, those seeking to enter do not need arms, and they come each year in their thousands, many of them from foreign lands in distant parts of the earth.

Times have surely changed for the better when the Castle, including the Black Tower, where in the past so many have suffered imprisonment and death, is used, as is fitting in the Capital City of the Land of Song, as a school of music.

The Shield of the Arms of Cardiff, which also includes the Welsh Leek, was granted in 1906. The Dragon was the symbol of the Roman cohort and, traditionally, was adopted by King Arthur in the wars with the Saxon invaders. The red banner with the three chevrons was carried by the Lords of Glamorgan.

APPENDIX A

The Roman Castrum

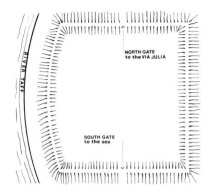

A.D. 76-250

Enclosing an area of approximately 7½ acres, banking 20′ high was built about half a mile in length, around a rectangular site slightly longer from north to south than from east to west. On the western side the banking bowed put in a gentle curve following the course of the River Taff. Dykes were probably dug outside the banking.

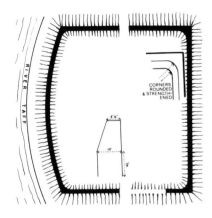

A.D. 250-300

Walls were built on the more exposed northern and eastern sides of the site, up to a certain height, without bastions, after which it is probable that similar walling was constructed on the western side and on the south, in part. These walls were 10′ thick except at the corners where they were strengthened by rounding them on the inner side, and there they attained a maximum thickness of 16′, and above the height of 9′, where by a series of intakes on the inner face of the wall a gradual reduction was affected to a minimum of 5′ 6″.

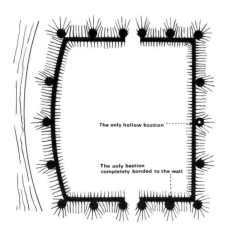

A.D. 300-350

The construction of the walls was continued. Bastions were built outside the walls to strengthen them and to provide platforms for catapults and other weapons. On reaching the height already attained by the walls, the bastions and walling were bonded together and the construction of both was continued simultaneously eventually reaching at least 17′ above the footings where by reason of the intakes the wall had been reduced in thickness to 5′ 6″.

The Norman Castle

A.D. 1090

Using the site of the old Roman Castrum, Fitzhamon built his Motte and Bailey castle. The Motte consisted of an artificial mound of about 40' high and 60 yards in diameter at the base, 33 yards across at the table level. Surrounded by a moat 30' wide and 20' deep it was surmounted by a timber stockade encircling a wooden tower. By digging ditches and using the soil the ruined wall was covered and the banking increased to a height of 27'.

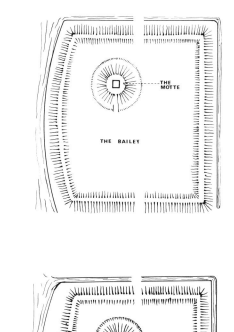

Between 1115 and 1147, Robert Consul replaced the wooden tower by a twelve sided Shell Keep of masonry 30' high with walls 6' thick enclosing an area 77' across. He also built a curtain wall to the west and south of the bailey and probably extended the outer moat to encircle the entire site.

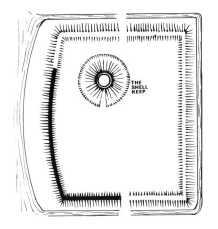

Between 1262 and 1295, Gilbert de Clare (II) built the Black Tower and a ward wall between it and the new Entrance Tower to the Keep. This divided the bailey into an inner and outer Ward. A North Wall was built joining the Keep to the West Wall which completed the enclosure of the inner ward, by then accessible only by way of a Castle Gateway and a postern gate. The inner ward was sub-divided into an inner and an outer Court. In the outer Ward were the Shire Hall, a Church and the Knight's Lodgings. Soil was removed from the inner ward and used to strengthen the banking around the outer Ward and possibly to fill in the southern moat

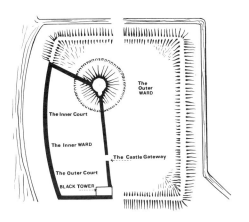

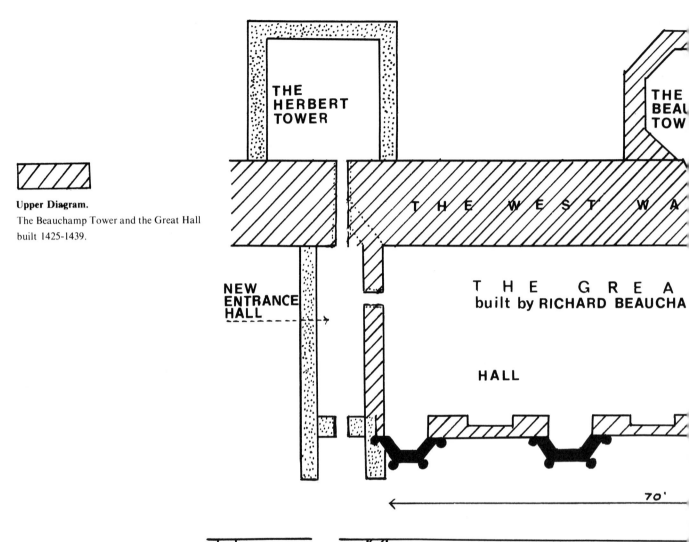

Upper Diagram.

The Beauchamp Tower and the Great Hall built 1425-1439.

THE HERBERT TOWER

THE BEAU TOW

THE WEST WA

NEW ENTRANCE HALL

THE GREA
built by RICHARD BEAUCHA

HALL

70'

Bay Windows added by Jasper Tudor 1488-1495.

DOMESTIC QUARTERS

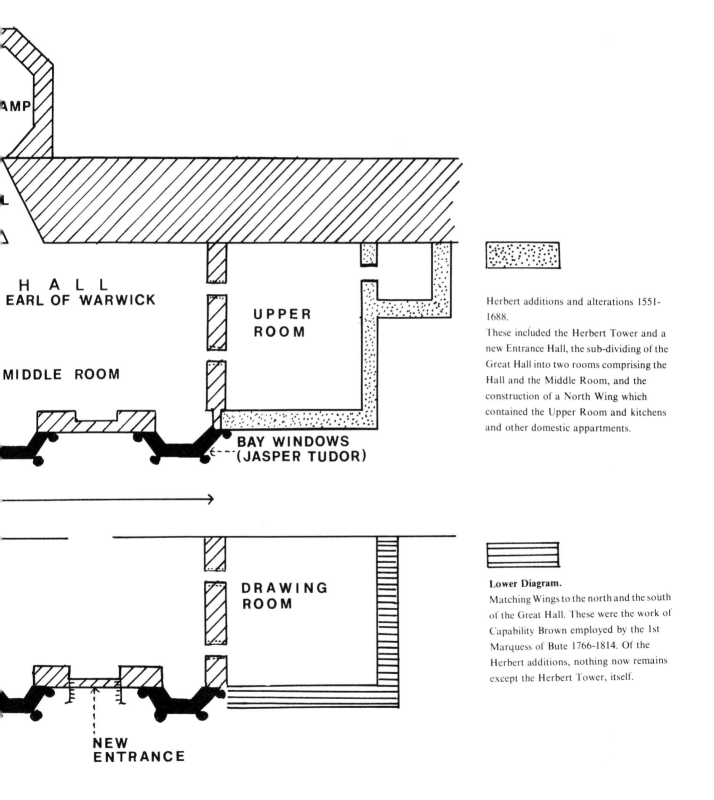

AMP

H A L L
EARL OF WARWICK

UPPER
ROOM

MIDDLE ROOM

BAY WINDOWS
(JASPER TUDOR)

Herbert additions and alterations 1551-1688.

These included the Herbert Tower and a new Entrance Hall, the sub-dividing of the Great Hall into two rooms comprising the Hall and the Middle Room, and the construction of a North Wing which contained the Upper Room and kitchens and other domestic appartments.

DRAWING
ROOM

NEW
ENTRANCE

Lower Diagram.
Matching Wings to the north and the south of the Great Hall. These were the work of Capability Brown employed by the 1st Marquess of Bute 1766-1814. Of the Herbert additions, nothing now remains except the Herbert Tower, itself.

The Changing Face of the southern half of the West Wall

As seen from outside the Castle in what is now Bute Park

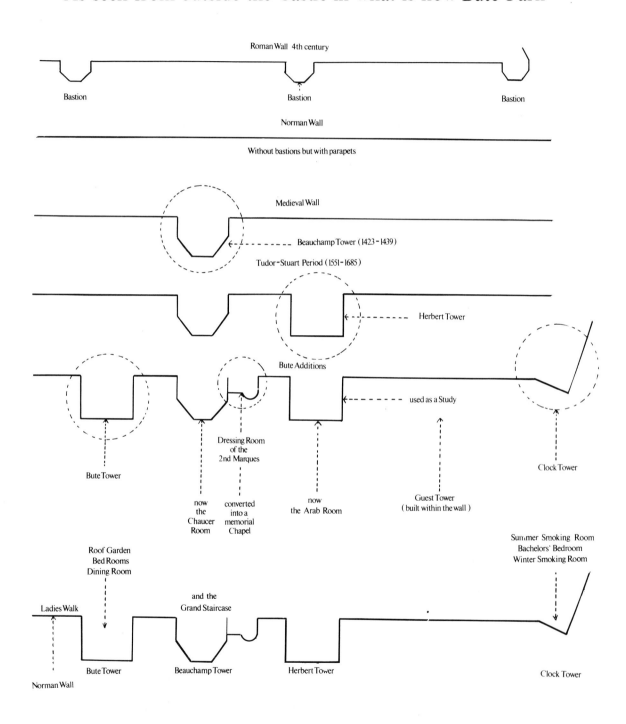

Roman Wall 4th century

Bastion

Bastion

Bastion

Norman Wall

Without bastions but with parapets

Medieval Wall

Beauchamp Tower (1423 – 1439)

Tudor – Stuart Period (1551 – 1685)

Herbert Tower

Bute Additions

used as a Study

Dressing Room
of the
2nd Marques

Clock Tower

Bute Tower

now
the
Chaucer
Room

converted
into a
memorial
Chapel

now
the Arab Room

Guest Tower
(built within the wall)

Summer Smoking Room
Bachelors' Bedroom
Winter Smoking Room

Roof Garden
Bed Rooms
Dining Room

and the
Grand Staircase

Ladies Walk

Bute Tower

Beauchamp Tower

Herbert Tower

Clock Tower

Norman Wall

Bibliography

A Bibliography of the History of Wales. Cardiff. University of Wales Press. 1960.

Boutell, Charles, *English Heraldry.* Gittings and Co., Ltd. 1902.

Burke, Sir Bernard, *Dormant, Abeyant, Forfeited and Extinct Peerages.* Harrison, 1883.

Donovan, *Excursions through South Wales. Volume I.* 1804.

Evans, C. J. O., *Glamorgan, Its History and Topography.* William Lewis Ltd. 1938.

Grant, John F. *Cardiff Castle. Its History and Architecture.* William Lewis Ltd. 1923.

Hindley, Geoffrey, *Medieval Warfare.* Wayland. 1971.

Jenkins, W. L. *History of Cardiff.* 1854.

Lever, Tesham, *The Herberts of Wilton.* John Murray. 1967.

Lloyd, Sir John E., *History of Wales from the Earliest Times to the Edwardian Conquest.* 2 Volumes. 1939.

Montagu-Smith, F. W. *The Royal Line of Succession.* Pitkin Pictorials Ltd.

Morris, J. E. *The Welsh Wars of Edward I.* Oxford. 1901.

Rees, William, *Cardiff. A History of the City.* Corporation of the City of Cardiff. 1969.

Rees, William, *An Historical Atlas of Wales from Early to Modern Times.* Cardiff. 1951.

Simpson, W. Douglas, *Castles in England and Wales.* Batsford. 1969.

Stroud, Dorothy, *Capability Brown.* Country Life. 1950.

Warner, Philip, *Sieges of the Middle Ages.* Bell. 1968.

Wheeler, R. E. M. *Prehistoric and Roman Wales.* Oxford. 1925.

Williams, Glanmor, *Owen Glendower.* Oxford. 1966.

Williams, W. N. and W. J. *The Castles of Wales.* St. Stephens Bristol Press.